THE MONTH
OF SAINT JOSEPH

San Jose con el Niño —Esteban Murillo

The Month of St. Joseph

OR

PRACTICAL MEDITATIONS FOR EACH
DAY OF THE MONTH OF MARCH

by

Abbe Berlioux

Translated from the French by
Eleanor Cholmeley

MEDIATRIX PRESS
MMXXII

ISBN: 978-1-957066-19-6

Originally published in 1888 by MH Gill and Son, Dublin.

The typography and editorial changes of this edition are ©Mediatrix Press, 2022. All rights reserved. No part of this work may be reproduced in electronic or physical formats without the express permission of the publisher, with the exception of quotations for review in journals, blogs, or classroom use. No part of this edition may be placed on archive.org

Nihil Obstat:
P. J. TYNAN, S. T. D.,
    Censor Theol., Deputatus.

Imprimatur:
✠ GULIELMUS J. WALSH,
    ARCHIEPISCOPUS DUBLINENSIS,
        HIBERNIÆ PRIMAS.

Pope Pius IX, by a rescript, dated June 11th, 1855, has granted an Indulgence of Three Hundred Days each day, to all those who perform, during the entire Month of March, the devotions of the Month of St. Joseph. These Indulgences can be applied to the Souls in Purgatory.

Mediatrix Press
607 E 6th Ave.
Post Falls, ID 83854
www.mediatrixpress.com

CONTENTS

FIRST DAY
The opening of the month.............. 1

SECOND DAY
Who is saint Joseph?.................. 7

THIRD DAY
The name of Joseph................... 13

FOURTH DAY
Joseph increased in wisdom and age. 19

FIFTH DAY
The election of Joseph 24

SIXTH DAY
Joseph and Mary..................... 29

SEVENTH DAY
Bethlehem........................... 34

EIGHTH DAY
The Epiphany........................ 39

NINTH DAY
The Circumcision.................... 44

TENTH DAY
The Presentation 49

ELEVENTH DAY
The Exile............................ 54

TWELFTH DAY
Joseph's life at Nazareth............... 60

THIRTEENTH DAY
Joseph loses and finds Jesus 65

FOURTEENTH DAY
St. Joseph's love for Jesus 71

FIFTEENTH DAY
St. Joseph the model of family life 76

SIXTEENTH DAY
St. Joseph our model for recollection 81

SEVENTEENTH DAY
St. Joseph, model of obedience 87

EIGHTEENTH DAY
St. Joseph, model of virginal chastity..... 92

NINETEENTH DAY
The feast of St. Joseph 98

TWENTIETH DAY
Joseph the model of prayer 104

TWENTY-FIRST DAY
St. Joseph, model of poverty 109

TWENTY-SECOND DAY
St. Joseph our model in suffering 114

TWENTY-THIRD DAY
St. Joseph, model of labor 120

TWENTY-FOURTH DAY
The happy death of Joseph 125

TWENTY-FIFTH DAY
St. Joseph, patron of a happy death 130

TWENTY-SIXTH DAY
St. Joseph in limbo. 136

TWENTY-SEVENTH DAY
The resurrection of Joseph. 142

TWENTY-EIGHTH DAY
St. Joseph in heaven 147

TWENTY-NINTH DAY
St. Joseph, patron of the universal church 152

THIRTIETH DAY
The excellence of devotion to St. Joseph . . 158

THIRTY-FIRST DAY
Practices in honor of St. Joseph. 164

LITANY OF ST. JOSEPH 171

MARCH DEVOTIONS 174

THE MONTH OF ST. JOSEPH

FIRST DAY

THE OPENING OF THE MONTH

I. Motives for sanctifying the month.
II. Means of sanctifying it well.

The First Point.—As during one month in the year we honor the mystery of the Infant Jesus, and during another the glories of Our Blessed Lady, it is fitting that we should pay some tribute of devotion to the man preeminently just who merited to be the Spouse of the Queen of Angels and the Foster-father of the Child Jesus.

You should then, O Christian soul, be especially devout to Saint Joseph during the month dedicated to his honor. You owe this to Jesus, who honored St. Joseph as his Father during thirty years of his life. You owe it to Mary, who honored Joseph as her

The Month of St. Joseph

Spouse and Guardian. You owe it to Joseph himself, who, after Jesus Mary, was preeminently the most just of men, and the most highly favored of the Saints. Finally, you owe it to yourself for, if you need a guide in the path of salvation, a comforter in your trials, a protector at the hour of death, St. Joseph will be to you an enlightened guide, a charitable comforter, a powerful protector. St. Bernard and St. Teresa say that "not only has he the power to help us in our spiritual and temporal necessities, but he obtains for us more than we ask for.

Pius IX of immortal memory, proclaimed him patron of the Universal Church, and recommended all Catholic nations to invoke this holy Patriarch with confidence. Let us then practice a devotion so pleasing to Jesus and Mary, and so salutary to ourselves. The month has now begun, and it will be to us like the Month of Mary, a month of benedictions, of graces, and of countless favors.

O Saint Joseph, thou who art my Father, I make thee an offering of this month; obtain for me the grace to spend it in a way that may tend to my sanctification.

Second Point.—The most efficacious way

The Month of St. Joseph

of spending this month is to make the virtues of our Holy Patron the subject of our daily meditations. "If you love St. Joseph," says St. Ambrose, "imitate his virtues;" they are in his heart like flowers in a fertile garden; each must be examined separately, in order fully to appreciate them. The knowledge thus obtained of the greatness of the virtues which distinguished St. Joseph, will induce us praise the Lord who has disclosed them us, and we shall be animated by a desire to imitate them.

Keep in your room a statue or picture of St. Joseph, and say your morning and night prayers before it. If possible hear Mass daily, or at least on Wednesdays, which is a day especially devoted to St. Joseph. In the course of the month receive Holy Communion in his honor, and offer this Communion to obtain through his intercession, the grace of a happy death and the relief of the souls in Purgatory.

Let these be our resolutions, and let us place them at the feet of St. Joseph, beseeching him to accept them, to bless them, and to help us to keep them.

O Mary our Mother! help us to love and honor thy virginal spouse as thou thyself didst love and honor him.

PRAYER

OBTAIN for me, I beseech thee, O St. Joseph, the requisite dispositions for spending this month well. Thou who didst guide Jesus so often when a child, guide and protect me during this month consecrated to thee. I will endeavor to be more zealous, I will imitate thy virtues and implore thy help. Grant me thy powerful protection, not only during the course of the month, but during my life and at the hour of my death. Amen.

EXAMPLE

In a parish of the Diocese of Grenoble, there lived a widow, who, though poor, endeavored to bring up her children in the practice of virtue; but her eldest son sadly disappointed her hopes, for being sent to Paris to finish his apprenticeship he led a wild life, and after some years returned home in shattered health. Like another St. Monica,

The Month of St. Joseph

his poor mother ceased not to weep and pray for the conversion of her prodigal son. It was her custom to celebrate the Month of St. Joseph every year together with her children, and this year they prayed with redoubled fervor in order to obtain his conversion. On the opening day of the month the young man entered the room where they were assembled, and asked the meaning of the little altar that had been erected. His mother replied that they were commencing the devotions of the Month of St. Joseph, and, she added, we are going to make it to obtain your conversion. The young man laughed, not only at the preparations for keeping the month, but at the intention for which it was to be offered. The next, and succeeding days, he returned at the same hour, laughing as usual at the piety of the little group; but after a few days he ceased to laugh, and appeared grave and thoughtful; he even listened to the chapter that was being read, and made the sign of the cross. The day after he returned, and was heard to ejaculate, "St. Joseph, have mercy on me," then turning to his mother, he said, "How unfortunate it is that I should have given up religion, and how happy you must be who practice it so well. I am resolved

The Month of St. Joseph

to change my life, and live like a Christian; and I trust St. Joseph, to whom you have prayed, will obtain grace and courage for me." Obeying the voice of God he approached the tribunal of confession, and received Communion with great devotion. After leading an exemplary life for some years he fell dangerously ill, and fortified by the last Sacraments his soul passed from this world to chant the mercies of God and the power of St. Joseph, for ever in heaven.

Let us also pray with confidence to this great Saint during this month, and he will obtain abundant graces for us.

SECOND DAY

WHO IS SAINT JOSEPH?

I. St. Joseph was just.
II. He was of the family of David.

First Point.—St. Luke's panegyric of the Blessed Virgin is expressed in but few words, *Jesus was born of Mary.* St. Matthew's praise of St. Joseph is still shorter; it is contained in three words, but they express everything: *Joseph was just; cum esset justus.* The Holy Ghost by these three words gives us the highest eulogium of this great Saint. According to the interpretation of the Doctors of the Church, the title of just signifies that Joseph was a man who possessed every virtue in an eminent degree, and that like Mary, he was the living copy of Jesus. Thus he was just towards God and full of faith, submission, confidence, and love of His divine majesty. He was *just* towards his neighbor, for he practiced all the spiritual and corporal works of charity; finally, he was *just* towards himself, for he did not neglect anything that could unite him to God, and preserve his soul from evil. It was then, by the practice of every virtue, by great holiness, and by an irreproachable life, that our glorious Patron merited the title of just, and for the same reason the Church designates him as most holy, Sanctissimum Joseph, a title which she bestows on no other saint. "Oh! how great," exclaimed St. Francis of Sales, "is the illustrious Joseph! well does he merit to be compared to the Palm, the king of trees, and it would even appear that he equaled in perfection, or possessed virtues to the same high degree, as the Blessed Virgin."

Enter into yourself, O Christian soul, and ask yourself this important question, Am I just? have I the justice which my vocation and state of life require; the justice that God has a right to expect from me in return for all the lights and graces I have received from Him? Are there not duties that I have almost entirely neglected, duties either towards God, towards my neighbor, or towards my own soul? Am I in such dispositions as would induce me to have recourse to St. Joseph, to obtain through his intercession a hunger and thirst for justice like that he possessed?

Second Point.—Joseph was of the family of David, that is to say, of the family chosen and consecrated for royalty. Amongst his ancestors could be reckoned Patriarchs, Princes, and Kings, and the throne had been promised as an everlasting heritage to the race of which he was the offspring. But what chiefly constituted the glory and greatness of St. Joseph is that he was of the favored family which was to give to the world the Messiah. He was of the same race as the Virgin Mary and Jesus her son. The time was now accomplished and the stem of Jesse would bud forth in him. Of his royal race the Desired of all nations was to be born, and he was to be His Father and Protector!

And we who belong to this royal Priesthood, inaugurated by the adopted Son of Joseph, do we fully understand the sublime height to which we have thus been raised. The Sacraments, but especially the Eucharist, identify us with the Divine Savior, and do we profit by it? Christian soul, recognize your dignity and examine seriously whether you have by the holiness of your life corresponded to your sublime vocation. O St. Joseph, obtain for us the grace to profit by the blessings which were showered upon you, and in which as Christians we participate.

PRAYER

O chaste Spouse of the Virgin Mary, a voice speaking to my heart seems to say, "Go to Joseph." I come, then, and prostrate before thee, I offer thee the first fruits of this month of graces, and I will endeavor to be more faithful and more zealous in thy service. Would that I had the same devotion for thee as the great St. Teresa, whose help I implore to spend this month well.

EXAMPLE

During the prevalence of a terrible epidemic, a zealous Priest entered a wretched hovel, where an old man lay dying of the contagion and covered with filthy rags. He

The Month of St. Joseph

was alone, a little straw served as a bed, and not a vestige of furniture was to be seen; for all had been sold the first days of his illness, to procure food. On the damp walls of the room hung two saws and a hatchet; these were all he possessed wherewith to gain a livelihood. "Be comforted," said the Priest; God gives you a great grace today, you are soon going to leave this world, where you have known nothing but sufferings."

"Nothing but sufferings!" replied the dying man, in a scarce audible voice; "you make a mistake; I took St. Joseph as my patron and model, and, like him, I have never murmured at my lot. I am a stranger to hatred and envy; my sleep has been peaceful; I was tired with my day's work, but I rested at night. The tools you see earned the bread that I eat with relish; I was poor, it is true, but St. Joseph was as poor as I was; and my health until now has been good. If I recover from this illness, which I do not expect, I will return to the wood-yard and continue to bless God who has taken such care of me."

The priest could scarcely conceal his surprise on hearing the poor man speak thus, but again addressing him, said: "Friend, although your life has not been the trial to

The Month of St. Joseph

you that I should have imagined it to have been, you must all the same resign yourself to die, for you must conform to the Will of God."

"I have known how to live," said the dying man, with a firm voice. "and I shall know how to die; thank God for the life he has given me, and for enabling me by death to come to Him."

Then receiving the last Sacraments with great devotion, this poor man, who had taken St. Joseph as his Patron and Model during life, calmly expired. Let us, like him, have recourse to this great Saint, and endeavor to imitate his virtues.

THIRD DAY

THE NAME OF JOSEPH

I. An honored name.
II. A saving name.

First Point.—It is the opinion of many of the Fathers of the Church that the name of Joseph was inspired by God. How great, then, must have been the love of God for this Patriarch, if the name that he was to bear before men and angels, was the Divine choice. This heavenly name, which in Hebrew signifies abundance and increase, was a happy omen of the treasures of grace which were to enrich the soul of this just man, and of the progress he was to make in perfection. St. Bernard says, that the interpretation of the name of Joseph, which means *augmentation*, should convince us what manner of man he must have been. His name was amongst the first that the Infant

Jesus lisped when in the arms of his Fosterfather, and Mary repeated it in her daily salutations.

Christian soul, pronounce with respect this name, which has emanated from the treasures of Divinity; this glorious name, which should always be associated in our minds with the sacred names of Jesus and Mary; this name which countless saints have venerated. Remember, also, that the name the Church has given you in Baptism, is taken from the calendar of the Saints, and thereby assures you a special Protector in Heaven. Be then very devout to your Patron Saint, bear his name with love and confidence, study his life, imitate his virtues, and daily invoke his assistance. Have you hitherto fulfilled this duty?

Second Point.—After the name of Jesus and that of the Queen of Heaven, what other name can assure us a more efficacious protection, than that of her spouse Joseph? It inspires confidence to the Christian soul, and is a source of the most abundant graces. A pious author calls it the "joy of Heaven, the hope of the earth, and the terror of Hell." Is it not sweeter than honey to the mouth, and more pleasant to the ear than the most melodious music? Yes, this venerated name possesses strength and virtue akin to that of the adorable names of Jesus and Mary; it is the joy of the exiled soul, it consoles it in its afflictions, enlightens it in its doubts, defends it against the enemies of its salvation, supports it at the dread hour of death, and opens to it the gates of Heaven. O Joseph, O name under the shield of which no one is permitted to lose courage or to despair.

Christian soul, may the name of Joseph, united to those of Jesus and Mary, be the first that you pronounce when you wake in the morning, and the last that you breathe at night, ere sleep closes your eyes. In life may this name be frequently on your lips, and at your last hour, when your soul is about to leave its earthly dwelling and pass into eternity, may your last words be those cherished names:

JESUS! MARY! JOSEPH!

The Month of St. Joseph

PRAYER

O Joseph, no lip can utter thy name without inflaming hearts with love for thee. Thy name is a prayer, and if I pronounce it with confidence, I shall obtain what I ask; it shall be ever on my lips during life, and at the hour of my death it will inspire me with confidence, and be my passport at that last hour.

EXAMPLE

In the year 1863, the Little Sisters of the Poor, wishing to establish their Order in Spain, opened a house for the aged poor in the town of Barcelona, and placed it under the protection of St. Joseph, to whom they gave the title of Purveyor of the House. At first the Sisters, owing, to the smallness of the building, could only accommodate women. One day, however, an old man of eighty knocked at the door and begged to be admitted.

The Month of St. Joseph

"I have come," said he, "to stay here."

"But," replied the Sister, "we are unable to receive men, for the house is too small." The old man heeded not the reply, but declared he would not go away. "What is your name?" asked the Superior.

"My name," said he, "is Joseph." The Sisters looked at each other, the name struck them and, moreover, it was Wednesday, a day especially dedicated to St. Joseph; so they resolved to keep him. But how were they to do? the old man was covered with vermin, and they had no change of clothes to give him.

"Go," said the Superior to one of the Sisters, "and see if you can beg some clothes in the town." Whilst they were speaking, the house door-bell rang, and an unknown person left a parcel. On opening it the Sisters found, to their surprise, a complete suit of men's clothes! The old man was overjoyed and the Sisters were still happier, and could not thank St. Joseph sufficiently for this mark of his protection. The house, under the auspices of the Holy Patriarch, has prospered ever since and, at the present time, affords shelter to two hundred old men, who end their days peacefully under the care of the

The Month of St. Joseph

Little Sisters of the Poor. Oh! how true it is that the name of Joseph brings happiness everywhere.

FOURTH DAY

JOSEPH INCREASED IN WISDOM AND AGE.

I. His Infancy.
II. His Manhood.

First Point.—Being destined by God for great things, St. Joseph, according to the pious belief of many of the Fathers of the Church, was purified before his birth from the stain of Original Sin. By means of this first grace, said the pious Gerson, the Lord destroyed, or at least diminished, in a considerable degree, the evil inclinations which are the bitter fruits of Original Sin, and He attached him irrevocably to Himself by the ties of love. Though Scripture is silent as regards the years of Joseph's youth, yet we may well believe that he sanctified them by the practice of every virtue, that he loved God in an eminent degree, that he was obedient and

The Month of St. Joseph

respectful to his parents, mild and gentle towards others, preserving unsullied the innocence of his soul, so that the learned Cornelius à Lapide, in speaking of him, called him an Angel rather than a man: *Fuit Angelus potiusquam homo.*

O Blessed Joseph, when I recall the years of my childhood, and compare them with thine, I am overwhelmed with sorrow. Alas! how many years have I lost. How late, O my God, have I loved Thee! I am resolved henceforth to do all in my power to repair the past by worthy fruits of penance. O St. Joseph, my Father, obtain for me this grace.

Second Point.—Like to a cloudless springtime the childhood of Joseph was passed in innocence, and as he grew to man's estate his virtues became still more conspicuous. He sought not the honors and riches of the world, but was content to remain humbly in the state of life in which Providence had placed him. He was a carpenter, and following his trade, he fulfilled all his duties towards God and his neighbor. Oh! how abundantly was grace showered on the soul of Joseph! Faithfully corresponding with it he advanced rapidly in the paths of justice. And was it not meet that he should be endowed with great sanctity, he to whose protection the God of Heaven was to confide His Only Son, and to whose guardianship was to be entrusted the Virgin of virgins.

What a lesson is the example of St. Joseph for young people, who, led away by the allurements of a voluptuous life, spend their best days in vice, reserving for God only the remnants of a life that is near its close. Fathers and mothers, place your children under the protection of the glorious Patriarch, to whom the Heavenly Father confided the care of His only Son. Beseech him to watch over their innocence and their avocations, and then they will, like him, advance in holiness and wisdom before God and before man.

PRAYER

Grant, O St. Joseph. that I may imitate the virtues thou didst practice in thy infancy and in thy youth. Watch over my heart, so that it may not yield to voluptuousness. Obtain that I ma be animated by the Spirit of God, and that the world may be crucified to me and I to the world. Amen.

EXAMPLE

On the fifth of November, 1865, a young man of 18, was carried in an unconscious state to the Hospital of La Motte Servieux. The Infirmarian asked if he had received the Sacraments.

"No, Sister," replied the unhappy father; "it is ten months since he went to confession." The doctors tried bleeding and other remedies, but all was of no avail, and at last they pronounced that life was extinct.

The Infirmarian Sister hearing that the youth's name was Joseph, declared that St. Joseph would not let any one die without the Sacraments, who bore his name. She then promised that should he recover he would receive Holy Communion every year on the feast of St. Joseph together with his father and mother. Night came on, but the invalid showed no sign of life. The Sister's confidence, however, did not waver, and towards five in the morning he became conscious, and asked to make his confession.

The Month of St. Joseph

St. Joseph who does not do things by halves, obtained his complete recovery, and he left the hospital, with a firm resolution to serve God more faithfully, and with feelings of the greatest gratitude towards his powerful Protector.

FIFTH DAY

THE ELECTION OF JOSEPH

I. How great was his mission.
II. In what way he performed it.

First Point.—Reflect that St. Joseph was chosen by God to be the Spouse of Mary, *Virum Mariæ*, and the Foster-father of Jesus: *Custos Domini sui*. He was appointed to watch over this Virgin and Child, he was to live with them, to provide for their necessities, and to die in their arms. Oh, how great was St. Joseph's vocation! A vocation worthy of the admiration of heaven and earth, a vocation which caused the celebrated Gerson to exclaim: "What honor can compare with this. that the Mother of God, the Queen of Heaven, should call Joseph her Spouse and Lord, that the Divine Word should call him Father, and should have obeyed him during thirty years! O Jesus, Mary, and Joseph, you form an earthly Trinity, which the Heavenly Trinity regards with delight." It was owing to the choice made of this glorious Patriarch, that St. Joseph has been raised above all other saints, and endowed with the graces and gifts that were necessary for the greatness of his mission. O Holy Joseph, let me unite with thee in thanking God for the great graces He bestowed upon thee.

Christian soul, in meditating on these consoling truths, remember that to you also has God confided Mary his Mother, and Jesus his Son, and that He has said to you, as He did to St. Joseph: Keep this treasure entrusted to you: *Depositum custodi.* Yes, be mindful of my Mother, show your love and your respect for her; for she loves you tenderly. Be mindful of my Son, whom you possess in the Blessed Eucharist, and be careful never to crucify Him again by sin.

Second Point.—Consider with what courage and fidelity St. Joseph fulfilled his mission. It was in order to correspond with God's designs that he applied himself to the practice of every virtue, accepted every sacrifice, that he endured the hardships of poverty, the sorrows of exile, and that he

The Month of St. Joseph

offered the labor of his hands, the sweat of his brow, and his whole life. Truly may it be said, that his motto was, All for Jesus, all for Mary!

He protected them, fed them, saved them at Bethlehem, in Egypt, and at Nazareth. In fine, he fulfilled his allotted task so well, that the Church calls him a faithful servant: *Fedelis servus.*

Christian soul, remember that we have all a mission to fulfil and duties to perform. Let us be faithful like St. Joseph. We shall have to answer to God for our eternity, for the gifts he has entrusted to us. Had we only our own souls to save, would not that be a great duty, a great responsibility; but, alas, how many other souls are there not depending upon ours! Oh, let us also be mindful of, and save the souls that have been entrusted to our care, so that we may one day hear those consoling words: "Well done, good and faithful servant, . . . enter thou into the joy of thy Lord" (Matt. 25:21.)

The Month of St. Joseph

PRAYER

Obtain for me, O Holy Joseph, the grace to be faithful to God's voice, and to accomplish in all things His will on earth. Grant that I may imitate thy fidelity to grace, and that regarding the praise or blame of the world with indifference, I may secure my eternal salvation.

EXAMPLE

A young man, the pride of his family, who lived in the city of Lyons, felt himself called to quit the world and enter religion. His parents grieved at the choice he had made, upbraided him, expostulated, and finally shed so many tears, that they succeeded in making him waver, and obtained the promise that he would at least defer for a time the execution of his design. Unhappy parents, to oppose what seemed so manifestly the will of God; and unhappy son not to have the courage to respond to God's call! Urged by his parents to lead a worldly

The Month of St. Joseph

life, in the hope that by so doing he would lose his vocation, the youth little by little neglected his religious practices, ceased frequenting the Sacraments, and gave himself up to a life of vice. After some time, ashamed of his excesses, and desirous to escape from the remonstrances of his parents, he left his home and enlisted in the army. Heart-broken and overwhelmed with remorse, his father and mother were afraid to pray, for they had taken their son from God and given him to the devil. At last, the thought occurred to have recourse to St. Joseph, to obtain forgiveness for themselves and the conversion of their son. With these intentions they began a Novena, and asked many of their friends to join in it. Their prayer was heard; St. Joseph obtained the desired conversion, and the youth returned to his father's house, a true penitent, edifying all by his exemplary life. Let ns learn from this example how all-important it is to hearken to God's voice, and correspond to the grace of our vocation.

SIXTH DAY

JOSEPH AND MARY

I. The love of Joseph for Mary.
II. The love of Mary for Joseph.

First Point—As Mary was destined to be the Mother of Jesus, it was fitting that she should have as a Spouse one whose pure life should help to conceal the adorable mystery of a God made man. St. Joseph was the Spouse thus privileged, *Virum Mariæ*, and the holy Patriarch testified his tender and respectful love for his immaculate Spouse by a watchful care and ready assistance in all her trials. According to Bossuet it was not external beauty, but the hidden and interior beauty of her soul, which formed her greatest ornament, and a pious author assures us, "that the love Joseph had for Mary was so exalted and purified in Divine love, that the human mind even with the aid of faith could not comprehend it."

Christian soul, endeavor to imitate this great model, and following the example of your glorious Patron St. Joseph, love Mary with all your heart. She was his Spouse, and she is your Mother: *Ecce Mater tua.* Remember that true devotion to the august queen of heaven is a mark of predestination, and that without her assistance it is morally impossible to succeed in the all-important work of salvation. Whatever is good has come to us and will still come to us through the hands of Mary. *Omnia per Mariam.* He who has found her has found life.

O blessed Joseph, obtain for me that true loving devotion towards your holy Spouse, which makes saints, and of which you yourself were the first and the most perfect example.

Second Point.—Mary is the Mother of beautiful love: *Mater pulchræ dilectionis.* Her love for God was greater than that of all the saints united, and her love for her neighbor was proportioned to her love for God. What, then, must have been her love for the holy Spouse chosen by God to be the inviolate witness of her virginity, and to protect her honor, and that of her divine Son? She would have loved him as the representative of God the Father and God the Holy Ghost, whose place he filled in her regard, and as the saint who bore the greatest resemblance to her Divine Son Jesus. Never did any spouse love more tenderly, or show greater respect, than Mary showed towards Joseph. In the words of St. Bernardine of Siena, "Mary and Joseph formed but one heart and soul; they were one in mind, one in love, one in all things." Oh, who else could have conceived such an ineffable, such an angelic affection! and how great a reward must it not have been to St. Joseph.

Christian soul, let us venerate the Spouse of Mary more than all the other saints, and let us never exclude him from the homage we offer to his immaculate Spouse. As Saturday is in a special manner dedicated to the Blessed Virgin, so is Wednesday consecrated to St. Joseph. If we are faithful in the observance of the Month of Mary, let us also be faithful in the observance of the Month of St. Joseph. These two devotions should not be separated; for they are the means of helping us to love Jesus. O Mary, we beseech thee to obtain for us a tender affection for

Joseph, thy virginal Spouse and our loving Father.

PRAYER

O Blessed Joseph, who wast raised to the dignity of Spouse of Mary, and who merited as such all our confidence, intercede for us, we beseech thee; remember that as her Spouse she can refuse thee nothing; ask her then to take us under her protection and to look upon us as her children. Amen.

EXAMPLE

Spiritual favors are not the only ones that St. Joseph obtains for those who have recourse to him. In the town of Roanne, in France, the Little Sisters of the Poor were burdened with a debt of two thousand francs; the time allowed for payment had nearly expired, and their purse was empty. The broken food they collected each day sufficed to feed their poor, but no help came to liquidate the debt of two thousand francs, "We must have recourse to St. Joseph," said one of the Sisters; "he alone can get us out of

The Month of St. Joseph

our difficulty, so let us begin a Novena to him," and writing their request on a slip of paper, they placed it at the foot of the statue of St. Joseph.

One day, before the Novena was finished, a lady, unknown to the community, who had been taken ill whilst staying at a hotel, sent for the Superioress and asked if she could have a room in their house. "We can take no one," said the sister, "but the aged poor, but I can tell you of an establishment where you will have better accommodation than any we could have given you."

"And do you accept alms," said the lady, "if any are offered you."

"Certainly," replied the Sister, "we have nothing else to support us." On receiving this answer the lady handed her a purse, and great was her surprise and gratitude, when on opening it she found it contained two thousand francs, the exact sum for which they had all prayed to St. Joseph.

SEVENTH DAY

BETHLEHEM

I. St. Joseph at the birth of Jesus.
II. The birth of Jesus in the Tabernacle.

First Point.—Obedient to the commands of the Emperor Augustus, Joseph, as is recorded in Scripture, went with Mary his Spouse from Galilee to Judea, from the town of Nazareth to that of David, which is called Bethlehem, to be enrolled. Finding no place in the inns on account of their poverty, they took refuge in a stable used for sheltering flocks at night. It was here that the Virgin of Israel miraculously brought forth her first-born Son. She wrapped Him in swaddling clothes, laid Him in the manger, and Joseph, prostrate in adoration, contemplated the Infant God with transports of joy.

Christian soul, learn today in the school of Joseph the heavenly lesson of contemplating Jesus. Imagine that you see the Infant God wrapped in swaddling clothes and laid upon straw in the manger. He weeps and He suffers, He is weak and poor in order to merit riches, greatness, and eternal glory for you. O Mary, O Joseph, instill into our hearts the sentiments that filled yours at the birth of the Incarnate Word.

Second Point. —St. Athanasius compares the Tabernacle which contains the Holy Eucharist to the manger in which the Infant Jesus was laid. The God whom we adore on the Altar was adored by Mary and Joseph in Bethlehem, the only difference being, that in the manger the sacred humanity of our Savior was mortal and subject to change, whereas on the Altar it is forever glorious and immortal. In a certain way we are more privileged than Joseph; he held Jesus in his arms, he could see, touch, and hear Him, all which things were external. How much more intimate is the intercourse that Communion establishes between Jesus and my soul! He comes to me, He enters my soul, He unites Himself to me, He in a certain way identifies Himself with me, in order to change me into Himself; so that it is not I who live, but Christ who liveth in me. Oh! what happiness and what an inexhaustible source of grace!

The Month of St. Joseph

How comes it then that we so rarely visit our divine Host and that we receive Him so seldom? He is in the Tabernacle out of love for man, and men neglect Him! He invites them to His table, and they refuse to come! No indeed, exclaimed St. Augustine, "love is not loved." *Amor non amatur.*

Christian soul, make an act of reparation to Jesus in the Holy Eucharist, and listen now to His loving call. O divine Emmanuel, victim of love, give us a great hunger and thirst for Thee, so that passing from the manger to the altar, from the Infant who smiles upon us to the God who gives Himself to us, we shall at length arrive at the Tabernacle of never-ending love, to the communion of life eternal!

PRAYER

I can share, O Blessed Joseph, in the happiness which thou didst experience at the birth of Christ; for the God made man whom thou didst adore in the stable at Bethlehem has become the life and food of our souls and a voluntary prisoner in our Tabernacles, But

The Month of St. Joseph

alas! neither my faith nor my love are equal to thine. Obtain for me then, O great Saint, that like thee I may find my happiness only in Jesus; for He alone is my treasure, my love, and my all.

EXAMPLE

A grenadier of the 29th regiment of infantry in the army of the Prince of Italy, had led a very irregular life, but more especially after entering the army. He not only laid aside the practice of his religious duties, but even the prayers he had learnt in childhood were neglected, with the exception of one Hail Mary and the following prayer to St. Joseph: "St. Joseph, who wert the father and guardian of the Holy Family, be also my father and protector, and obtain for me a happy death." These were the only religious acts which he performed, and he never omitted reciting these two prayers daily. Strange as it may appear, he had great confidence in Saint Joseph, and frequently repeated his name when anything troubled or annoyed him. At the battle of Laybach, in1809, he was wounded in the leg by a cannon ball, and being unable to stand was

The Month of St. Joseph

carried to the nearest house. His first exclamation was: "Saint Joseph, Saint Joseph"; and in the midst of his sufferings these were the only words he uttered. An exiled French Priest, who was in the adjoining room, hearing his groans accompanied by the exclamations, "Saint Joseph, Saint Joseph", thought the wounded soldier might be glad of religious assistance. He, therefore, hastened to his bedside, and finding him eager to make his confession, administered the last Sacraments, and shortly after the grenadier expired invoking the name of Joseph.

EIGHTH DAY

THE EPIPHANY

I. Joseph and the Magi.
II. Visits to the Blessed Sacrament.

First Point.—A short time had elapsed after the birth of Jesus, when Joseph saw the Kings of the East come to the stable. Guided by a miraculous star they had reached Bethlehem, and entering the place where the Child was laid had prostrated themselves before the newborn Savior, offering Him gifts of gold, frankincense, and myrrh. What must have been the joy and happiness of the holy Patriarch on this great day, when he welcomed the Magi and presented the divine Infant to them to receive the homage of their adoration, and when he blessed the goodness of God, who in the persons of the Wise Men offered salvation to all mankind without distinction of race or origin. Rejoice, O Joseph, this Infant which is the object of your care, will soon be known and adored by the whole world. Already the Jews and Gentiles, represented by the shepherds of Palestine and, the Magi of the East, acknowledge Him for their King, their Savior, and their God. Already has begun the accomplishment of those prophetic words: 'Let all the angels of God adore Him." (Hebrews, 1:6.)

Christian soul, rejoice with Joseph and Mary at this glorious manifestation of Jesus, and thank God for having called you like the Magi to the knowledge of His Divine Son in preference to so many others who have not even heard His name. Endeavor to follow the example of the Wise Men by making Jesus known and loved. Be the guiding star to others, bringing Him faithful adorers, and then St. Joseph will in return conduct you one day to his Son in the realms of eternal glory.

Second Point.—The happiness which the Magi experienced was indeed great; the Infant Jesus allowed them to pay Him homage and showered His favors on them.

The Month of St. Joseph

"For the gold they offered," says a pious author, "they received the gift of wisdom; for the frankincense the gift of prayer; and for the myrrh the knowledge of the cross." Are we less privileged than they were? Cannot we also visit Jesus, contemplate Him in His humiliations, offer Him our hearts, and solicit His blessings? Is He less loving and less rich in the tabernacle than in the stable in which He was born? Faith tells us He is truly in this prison of love, that He waits for us there, that His heart is open to receive all our requests, that His hands are filled with graces which He is desirous to bestow upon us; "Come to me." said He, "all you that labor and are burdened, and I will refresh you" (Matt. 11:28).

Christian soul, resolve never to pass a day without making a short visit to our loving Savior in the Sacrament of His love. St. Teresa, St. Catharine of Genoa, St. Aloysius would have remained all their lives at His feet, had it been possible, and "St. Francis Xavier often passed whole nights in adoration before the Blessed Sacrament. In a word, devotion to Jesus in the Blessed Sacrament has always been the characteristic devotion of the saints. Let it also be yours.

The Month of St. Joseph

Seek not for consolation elsewhere; a visit to the Blessed Sacrament will give you rest if fatigued, it will revive your hopes if you are downcast, and you will realize the truth of the words, *He who has Jesus possesses all things.*

PRAYER

I thank Thee, O Lord, a thousand times for having called me like the Wise Men to the knowledge of our Lord Jesus Christ. Grant me, I beseech Thee, through the intercession of St. Joseph, grace to be faithful to my vocation. I will cherish this most precious gift, and like the Wise Men, I will persevere in the true faith until death.

EXAMPLE

During the plague which scourged the city of Lyons in 1638, a great number of the inhabitants were either preserved from it or recovered when attacked by means of the intercession of St. Joseph. The child of a

The Month of St. Joseph

lawyer, a boy seven years old, was attacked by the plague and had all the symptoms which in such cases usually denote the near approach of death. The father, who was a good and pious man, did not lose confidence, but invoked St. Joseph, and made a promise that if his child recovered he would for nine days hear Mass in the church dedicated to him, burn wax candles in his honor, and place a votive inscription commemorating the favor obtained through his intercession. In the meantime the physicians continued their visits to the sick child, whose state became so much worse that they ordered him to be taken to the Lazaretto, saying he had scarcely two hours to live. The order was promptly executed, but no sooner had the child reached the pest-house than he was perfectly cured. The father, overwhelmed with gratitude to his glorious benefactor, fulfilled immediately the vow he had made.

NINTH DAY

THE CIRCUMCISION

I. Joseph gives the name of Jesus.
II. Devotion to this Holy Name.

First Point.—Consider the glory of St. Joseph on the day of Circumcision, as Head of the Holy Family and adopted Father of the Divine Infant, his office was to give Him the most holy and powerful of all names. God had, through the angel Gabriel, revealed this adorable name, and had signified to him all its greatness. "Thou shalt call His name Jesus" (Luke, I. 31), and prostrating himself before the Infant God, the holy Patriarch inwardly exclaimed: "Receive, O Lord, receive this sacred Name before which every knee shall bow in heaven, on earth, and in hell. It shall be as a sweet oil which shall be poured into the recesses of my soul." *Oleum effusum nomen tuum.* It was then the glorious

The Month of St. Joseph

Patriarch who had the signal privilege of giving to the Incarnate Word this blessed name and of being the first to pronounce the name of Jesus, which expresses all our hopes. From that moment he had the consolation of repeating this Holy Name many times in the day during the space of the thirty years that he conversed with the Son of God. O blessed Joseph, I rejoice at the thought that Thou wert chosen to give this great Name to the Savior of men! If St. Paul became a vessel of election destined to carry this Name to the kings and nations of the earth, with how much more reason were you elected, you who gave it to the Divine Infant, and repeated it to men and angels. Obtain for me, I beseech thee, O great Saint, the grace of a tender devotion to the name of Jesus.

Second Point.—Following the example of St. Joseph, let us always pronounce the Name of Jesus with the threefold sentiment it inspires. *First*, with confidence, for we have in Jesus the most tender of Fathers, the most faithful of friends, the most powerful protector; and He Himself assures us, that all that we ask of God in His name shall be granted unto us. *Secondly*, let us pronounce it with gratitude for it was for our salvation that the Son of God took the name of Jesus; and this name recalls to our remembrance the labors, the humiliations, the sufferings He underwent to ensure our eternal happiness. *Thirdly*, let us pronounce this name with love. St. Francis of Sales writing to a holy widow said: "Oh! how sweet is the name of Jesus! but to pronounce it properly we should have a heart burning with love." "All is insipid to me," said Saint Bernard, "if devoid of the name of Jesus; all that you speak of appears cold and has no charm, if I hear not the name of Jesus. Yes, Jesus is honey to my mouth, melody to my ears, and joy to my heart."

Christian soul, in all your troubles, in all your dangers, invoke the name of Jesus; it will be your riches, your support, your salvation; O Joseph, obtain for us the grace of true devotion to this Holy Name which was everything to you. O Jesus! save us through your name. *In Nomine tuo salvum me fac.*

The Month of St. Joseph

PRAYER

O Holy Joseph, grant that like thee I may find strength and comfort in invoking the sacred name that thou didst give to the world's Redeemer. Grant that when I pronounce this name; it may be with faith, respect, and love. May the sacred name of Jesus be my consolation in my trials, my light in my doubts, my strength in my temptations, and my last word at the hour of my death,

EXAMPLE

The Rev. Father Bouveret, Parish Priest of Byans, relates the following incident in a letter dated September 20th, 1871. During the last seventeen years a very bigoted Protestant lived in my parish. Whenever a favorable opportunity occurred it was made use of to induce him to renounce his errors and join the Church, but he rejected every advance that was made to him. Last August he fell dangerously ill, and friends having begged me to go to him, I again urged him to

The Month of St. Joseph

abjure Protestantism. He refused me so decidedly that, seeing the utter uselessness of saying anything more on the subject, I rose to leave, saying, I am now going to celebrate Mass, I shall pray earnestly for you, and do you pray also that God may direct you what to do. I spoke also to the different members of his family, asking them, as they were converts, to join me in praying for him. Before beginning Mass, I recommended the dying man in a special manner to St. Joseph, placing him under his protection; I lit a candle before his altar, and I made a promise, that if he converted my Protestant, I would publish the fact. St. Joseph granted my prayer. At the end of Mass I went again to the dying man and found him quite changed; be listened to my instruction, made his abjuration and received eagerly the last Sacraments. There was indeed no time to lose, for two hours later he expired, but he died a good and fervent Catholic.

TENTH DAY

THE PRESENTATION

I. Joseph and Mary present Jesus in the Temple.
II. Offering of the Holy Sacrifice.

First Point.—Consider St. Joseph accompanying the Blessed Virgin to the Temple to offer with her the Infant Jesus to the Eternal Father, forty days after His birth, as was enjoined by the Law of Moses. As head of the Holy Family Joseph could offer nothing more precious than the Divine Infant, who had become his foster Son, and whom he loved with the most ardent love. It was, however, this precious offering that he laid upon the altar and gave to God generously and without reserve. Enlightened by the Prophecy of Simeon as to the future of this adorable Infant, and with his soul overwhelmed with sorrow, we may well

The Month of St. Joseph

believe that he offered it together with Mary to be one day immolated for the salvation of the world. It would seem that he heard the voice of the God of Abraham saying: "Take thy only Son whom thou lovest . . . . and offer him as a holocaust" (Gen. 22:2); and he answering said, Lord I will do it, because Thy Law is engraven on my heart; yes, receive this Unspotted Lamb, whose blood will one day wash away the sins of the world. I unite my sacrifice to that of Jesus, my adopted Son, I offer myself to Thee, O my God, to love and serve Thee alone and to accomplish Thy holy will. Oh, what a generous offering was that which Joseph made and how acceptable it must have been in God's sight.

Christian soul, God asks you to offer Him your daily actions; it is not only a holy practice, but a real duty; for you were only created to serve God. Fulfil then this duty with fidelity, and every morning on waking say: My God, I offer Thee my heart and all the thoughts, words, actions and sufferings of this day for Thy greater glory.

Second Point.—Let us not forget that when we assist at the Holy Sacrifice of the Mass, we, like St. Joseph, offer Jesus to His

The Month of St. Joseph

Eternal Father. Together with the Priest we say: "Accept, O Holy Father, this unspotted Host which we offer unto Thee . . . . for all faithful Christians both living and dead." Do we assist this August Sacrifice with dispositions similar to those that animated St. Joseph when he offered Jesus in the Temple? Do we reflect that according to what St. Liguori says, one single Mass gives more glory to God than do or can do the united merits of all the saints; and the fruits of one single Mass are greater than any we could ever derive from a life spent entirely in prayer. In the Mass we unite ourselves to the great Victim, to offer ourselves and all that belongs to us to God. We should, as the "Imitation of Christ" says, grieve that so few know how to appreciate this saving Mystery which rejoices Heaven and preserves the world.

Let us, O Christian soul, make a firm resolution to hear Mass in future oftener and with greater devotion. That Chalice of Salvation which is offered to the Divine Majesty contains everything; adoration, thanksgiving, expiation, help for the living, relief for the dead. O Mary, O Joseph, grant that I may imitate you, and that henceforth,

The Month of St. Joseph

when I assist at Mass, I may picture to myself that you are by my side.

PRAYER

Great Saint, who wert the first after Mary to offer Jesus to His Eternal Father on the altar of thy heart, lend me your feelings of faith, love, and piety, when I am present at the Holy Sacrifice of the Mass. What abundant fruits would be mine if my hands, lips, and heart were more pure. I will in future picture to myself when hearing Mass, that thou art near me, and uniting myself to thy feelings of love, I shall pray with greater fervor.

EXAMPLE

Some years ago a young man devoid of all religious feeling, who lived in the city of Turin, bought a pennyworth of tobacco which was wrapped in a piece of printed paper. To while away the time he began to read what was on the paper. It happened to be a prayer to Saint Joseph, to obtain a happy

The Month of St. Joseph

death, and although he hardly understood the meaning, it made an impression on him, and the thought recurring to his mind, he took the paper from his pocket and read it again. His companions, whose curiosity was excited, tried to get the paper from him, but he hid it and joined in their games. As soon as he found himself alone, he took out his paper; for an indescribable impression had been left on his mind the first time he read it. After reading it again and again, he ended by learning it by heart, and often found himself repeating it unconsciously.

Though the homage he thus paid to St. Joseph was as it were involuntary, yet it did not pass un rewarded. St. Joseph touched his heart, and enlightening his understanding, the truths of religion presented themselves so forcibly to him, that he sought a priest and put himself under instructions. His after-life edified all who knew him, and he persuaded many to let no day pass without praying to St. Joseph for a happy death.

ELEVENTH DAY

THE EXILE

I. The flight into Egypt.
II. The sojourn in Egypt.

First Point.—Stillness like the calm of Heaven reigned at Nazareth, when suddenly in the middle of the night the angel of the Lord appeared to Joseph saying: " Arise and take the Child and His Mother, and fly into Egypt . . . . for it will come to pass that Herod will seek the Child to destroy Him" (Matt. 2:13). What a trial was this to Joseph's faith! his Son, the Son of the Most High, was pursued by a tyrant, who had sworn to take His life. Even the angel appeared alarmed at the Infant's danger; and "it would seem," said a Holy Father, "that there was terror in Heaven before it spread upon earth." But on Joseph's part how great was his submission; he obeyed without delay, he took the child Jesus in his arms and with Mary set out for Egypt. Represent to yourself the Holy Family in this precipitate flight ; follow them through the unknown countries and sandy deserts that they traversed with no other food than what they received miraculously, or that was given to them as an alms; without any other guide but abandonment to divine Providence; with no shelter but the vault of Heaven, and this for a distance of a hundred and fifty leagues. Who, exclaimed Albert the Great, can express the greatness of these tribulations: *Quæ major tribulatio?* How true it is that Jesus came into the world to save us by the cross. Hardly is He born but He carries it Himself, and makes both His Mother and His foster-father bear it in order to associate them in the work of the Redemption. "Wherever Jesus enters," said Bossuet, "He enters with the cross, and with it He brings *thorns*, which He gives to all those He loves."

Accept then, O Christian soul, the cross that the Master presents to you; it is a token of love, the sign of salvation, the key of Heaven. "Let us love our crosses," said St. Francis of Sales, "for they are all made of gold."

Second Point.—When the Holy Family reached the land of Egypt, Joseph, according to tradition, settled in a town called Heliopolis, and remained there about seven years. Who can form an idea of the privations, sufferings and humiliations he endured during this long exile! St. Bonaventure, Mary of Agreda, and other writers are of opinion that not only St. Joseph but Jesus and Mary suffered the greatest poverty and misery, and according to a pious author the child Jesus when pressed by hunger would ask Joseph for bread and Joseph had none to give Him. Not only had St. Joseph to bear this trial but that also of seeing the Savior so offended by this Pagan nation, where all things was as God except God Himself; for idolatry under the most revolting forms accompanied by the grossest vices reigned around. Nevertheless, in the midst of these trials the courage of the holy Patriarch never failed. He found in the companionship of Jesus and Mary the comfort he needed to bear patiently the severities of exile. To be with Jesus, says the author of the "Imitation," is to be in a paradise of delights.

Christian soul, the world is to us a land of

exile, a vale of tears, where we mourn and weep without ceasing, *Gementes et flentes.* Let us learn from our holy protector, that it is by a close union with Jesus and Mary that we shall obtain strength, support, and consolation. At the same time our hearts should be fixed on our Heavenly country where we shall rejoice eternally with Jesus, Mary, and Joseph. Let us often repeat the words: a moment of suffering, an eternity of happiness!

PRAYER

O Blessed Joseph, who didst accompany the Child Jesus in His journeyings, guide and protect me in all my ways wheresoever I am. Never permit me to stray from the paths of virtue or to lose the company of Jesus and Mary; keep me from danger, strengthen me in my labors, until I come to the land of eternal rest. Amen.

EXAMPLE

A saintly Religious was inspired by the Blessed Virgin to beg through the intercession of her holy Spouse, Saint Joseph, grace to perform her spiritual exercises with fervor. This Religious was much troubled with violent temptations every time she began to meditate on the truths of eternity, and the violence of these temptations was such, that she gave way to fear and discouragement. In her anguish she had recourse to the Blessed Virgin. whom she besought to obtain peace of mind for her, so that she might pray with tranquility and devotion. "O Mary," she exclaimed, "if thou wilt not obtain the favor I ask for, at least inspire me to have recourse to the saint most dear to thee, and from whom I may implore this grace with confidence." Scarcely had she uttered this prayer when she felt her heart overflow with peace and spiritual sweetness; at the same time it was intimated to her that St. Joseph, the beloved Spouse of Mary, was dear to her above all the other saints, and on account of his transcendent virtues, worthy of being the Father and Master of all who wish to lead an interior and spiritual life.

The Month of St. Joseph

From that moment the Religious placed herself under his protection, and soon experienced the efficacy of his powerful intercession by being freed from all the temptations which had till then molested her; and whenever she felt the least return of them, she had only to invoke her good Father who immediately obtained for her peace of mind and interior recollection.

TWELFTH DAY

JOSEPH'S LIFE AT NAZARETH

I. His daily life.
II. His interior life.

First Point.—Herod being dead, the angel of the Lord appeared again to Joseph, and said unto him, "Arise, take the Infant and its mother, and go into the hand of Israel" (Matt. 2:20). The Holy Family then went back to the house in Nazareth where the mystery of the Incarnation had taken place. Contemplate Joseph during the twenty years he passed in this humble dwelling. The life he led had nothing in it to attract public attention, nothing that appeared extraordinary. Even Scripture is silent regarding it. At that time there were illustrious men m Jerusalem and Rome, whose fame filled the world, for it was the age of Herod and Augustus. But no one was aware of what was passing in Joseph's workshop at Nazareth. All who knew Joseph saw only a humble workman, a carpenter busy with the work that his position and the support of Jesus and Mary required from him. But under such an ordinary appearance what treasures of grace and sanctity were hidden! Joseph did all things well, his ordinary actions were full of merit before God, because they were done with a pure intention and great charity.

Christian soul, learn from this that sanctity does not consist in appointments to high places and in doing great things, but in sanctifying the ordinary actions of our lives by performing them from supernatural motives. All that is not done for God is lost for eternity. How many persons are there who give themselves no end of trouble, and who at the last Judgment will appear with empty hands. Be faithful then in little things, it is the secret of perfection and the safest way to reach heaven.

Second Point.—St. Joseph is a perfect model of the interior life. His days were passed in his humble workshop, and it was only when his avocations obliged him, that he appeared in public. God bestowed his graces on him and enriched him with the most precious treasures. Like Mary he kept them in his heart and revealed them not. Oh what countless merits and virtues did not this holy Patriarch amass in the retired life he spent afar from creatures and the turmoil of passions, in close union with Jesus and Mary. Words cannot express, says a pious author, the wonderful qualities with which the soul of Joseph was endowed, but at the Judgment day we shall know them, and it is then that these supernatural splendors which humility concealed will be made manifest, and all will acknowledge the greatness of the sanctity which had been hidden under the veil of an obscure life.

Christian soul, learn then the happiness and excellence of an interior life and intimate union with God. If we would seek earnestly after perfection we must, like our glorious Model, live lives that are hidden and unknown. *Ama nesciri.* "With desolation is all the land made desolate; because there is none that considereth in the heart" (Jer. 12:11). O God of goodness and of love, grant that following Joseph's example we may walk always in Thy presence.

The Month of St. Joseph

PRAYER

O glorious St. Joseph, thou who didst watch over and protect the Holy Family of Nazareth, watch over and protect us also. O great saint, obtain for us the grace to fear the allurements of the world and to hear and obey the voice of God when He speaks to our hearts. Amen.

EXAMPLE

A student belonging to the College of Fano was in the year 1855 taken dangerously ill. Several doctors were called in, but their remedies gave no relief, and he seemed gradually sinking. After a further consultation the physicians declared that nothing could save him, and moreover, that as death might occur at any moment it would be advisable to administer the last Sacraments. His confessor knowing that nothing more could be hoped for from man, advised him to put his trust in St. Joseph, and to pray to him with great confidence. He also recommended him to have seven Masses offered in honor of the seven joys and the seven sorrows of the great patriarch, and to receive Communion on the Feast of the Patronage which was near at hand. Furthermore, he suggested that a statue of the saint should be placed in his room, and that on the eve of the feast he should burn two wax candles before it. All this the student promised to do, and St. Joseph was not unmindful of these testimonies of confidence and love. The very day the promises were made a change was perceived in the invalid; the dangerous symptoms disappeared, and before many days had elapsed he was entirely restored to health. The case was the more remarkable as many members of his family had died from the same complaint.

THIRTEENTH DAY

JOSEPH LOSES AND FINDS JESUS

I. His grief.
II. His joy.

First Point.—According to the Gospel Joseph and Mary went every year to Jerusalem for the Feast of the Passover, and when Jesus had attained the age of twelve years He accompanied. them in the journey. When the solemn festival was over, Joseph and Mary, together with other pilgrims, took the road that led to Nazareth, Joseph walking with the men, and Mary with the women, as was the custom of their country. Neither of them was uneasy as to where Jesus was, for Joseph supposed him to be with His Mother, and Mary believed He had accompanied Joseph. When the first day's journey was over and they joined each other in the evening, they became aware that Jesus was not with them.

The Month of St. Joseph

It is not difficult to imagine the grief of Mary and Joseph; Jesus, their love, their consolation, their life, was not there. In vain did they seek for Him asking all whom they met if they had seen Him: *Dolentes quærebamus te*; and thus passed two whole days.

We also lose Jesus, but in two different ways: first by sin, and then His loss is a punishment; Jesus leaves a heart where the devil has entered, He vanishes and leaves the cruel tyrant of hell to reign there. What a terrible misfortune is this, one that should be lamented with tears of blood. O Joseph, preserve us from so dreadful a fate; O Jesus, stay forever with us.

We lose Jesus also by interior dryness and desolations, and then it is a trial. We thought Jesus was with us, but He has disappeared. Afflicted soul, do not despair; Jesus is not lost forever; you will soon find Him again. Bear this trial with patience, it will prove more useful to you than sensible consolations. Strengthen your will by prayer, persevere in your different exercises of piety, have recourse with confidence to Mary and Joseph, and they will help you to find calm of mind, peace, and interior joy.

The Month of St. Joseph

Second Point.—After three days' anxious search Joseph and Mary find Jesus in the temple of Jerusalem. Jesus, according to the Gospel, was in the Temple, sitting in the midst of the doctors, hearing them and asking them questions. And all that heard Him were astonished at His wisdom and His answers (Luke, 11:46, 47). What a moment of joy must this not have been after these cruel sufferings. Joseph finds his well-loved Jesus, whose loss had caused him such affliction. We find Him not in a worldly assembly, but in the House of God, in the midst of the doctors, commanding at the age of twelve years this admiration of the Elders of Israel, and revealing His Divinity for the first time to those who were willing to acknowledge it. Without doubt this was one of the happiest moments in the glorious Patriarch's life. He called the child Jesus, received Him into his arms, and would have explained in the words of Scripture: "I have found Him whom my soul loveth; I hold Him and will not let Him go" (Cant. 3:4).

Having in vain sought Jesus, Joseph at last found Him in the Temple, and it is there also that you, O Christian soul, will find Him. He cannot go away, He is chained to the

Tabernacle by links of love. It is there that He gives His divine lessons, there He speaks to hearts and appeals to them. Let us often go to Him to learn the science of the saints and the road to Heaven. One word spoken to our inmost hearts will teach us more than is contained in meditations or spiritual reading books; and of what use would books and reflections be, if God spoke not to our hearts.

PRAYER

O glorious St. Joseph, obtain for me the grace to watch over myself so that I may never risk losing Jesus. But should this misfortune be mine, obtain for me your courage and perseverance, so that I may seek Him until I find Him again; and grant that I may never more be separated from Him, but remain united to Him until death. Amen.

EXAMPLE

Many are the instances of St. Joseph's solicitude to aid and console his devout clients at the hour of death, sometimes even visibly and accompanied by the most holy Virgin. The following incident is an illustration of this truth.

In the Novitiate of the Society of Jesus at Chieri, there was a lay-brother named Dominic Jemi, who was dying of consumption. He was a Religious of extraordinary virtue and remarkable for his obedience, humility, union with God, and his special devotion to St. Joseph. During his illness he was most patient and resigned, and he bore his sufferings with a cheerfulness which edified all who saw him. As the hour of death drew nigh, the cell of this good Religious seemed changed into a little paradise, so perpetually was he occupied in expressing the most ardent affections of his heart, sometimes to Jesus crucified, or to the Sacred Heart, the Blessed Virgin, and to His special patron, St. Joseph. The night preceding his death it seemed that the Blessed Virgin and St. Joseph appeared to him; making an effort beyond his strength he endeavored to raise his hands and bow his head towards the spot where he saw them, exclaiming repeatedly, in transports of joy: "Brethren, do you see the Blessed Virgin and St. Joseph? Let us kneel down to honor and

The Month of St. Joseph

invoke them." After praying with much fervor for himself, for those around him, and for the absent, he calmly expired.

    This happy death, at which Mary and her glorious Spouse St. Joseph assisted, occurred on the 10th of December, 1828.

FOURTEENTH DAY

ST. JOSEPH'S LOVE FOR JESUS

I. A tender love.
II. A generous love.

First Point—When St. Joseph became acquainted with the mystery of the Incarnation of the unborn Son of Mary, God at the same moment enkindled in Joseph's heart the most tender love for Him. It would seem as though the love of the Eternal Father for His Son passed in some measure into the heart of the Holy Patriarch. Joseph's love was not then a merely human love, but a supernatural love, pure and tender, reverent and adoring. According to St. Bernardine of Siena, the smiles, the words, and fond caresses of the Infant God enkindled feelings of the deepest love in Joseph's heart. "Oh, what great love," exclaimed St. Liguori, "did not Joseph feel for the Holy Infant when he carried Him in his arms and pressed Him to his heart." Yes, truly, we may well believe that no saint, except Mary, has ever loved Jesus as Joseph loved him.

Christian soul, how happy you would be if you could love Jesus as the Spouse of Mary loved Him, if you could love Him as did St. Francis of Sales, who was wont to exclaim in the words of an earlier saint, "To love or to die." Or, like the saintly Curé of Ars, who used to say, "Our good God created the little birds to sing, and they sing; He created man to love Him, and men love Him not." O sweet Jesus, give me the ardent love of Thee with which Saint Joseph was inflamed and I shall have nothing more to wish for on earth.

Second Point.—The love of Joseph for Our Lord was not only a real, it was also a very generous love. "True Charity," said a saint, "is known by its works." With the exception of the Blessed Virgin, where is the saint who has labored more for His glory than did St. Joseph? The Apostles preached his Gospel, the Martyrs sealed it with their blood, the Doctors of the Church have labored for Him, charitable souls have fed His poor; but what they each did for His mystic body, St. Joseph did for the Redeemer Himself. It was to save

The Month of St. Joseph

Him from persecution that he braved the dangers of the desert and fled with him into Egypt; it was for Him that he went from Judea to Galilee, to escape the jealous fury of Herod's son; it was to feed Him that he labored with the sweat of his brow. His whole life was consecrated to his Incarnate God. Could he have done more or what more convincing proof could he have given of his great love?

Consider, Christian soul, that real love for Jesus consists in suffering for Him and in sacrificing yourself with Him and for Him. "If any man will follow me let him deny himself, and take up his cross and follow me" (Matt. viii. 34); and the "Imitation of Christ" tells us that a life of love is never without suffering, and whoever is not ready to suffer is not worthy to be a disciple of a Crucified God. O sweet Jesus, how many love Thee for their own pleasure, but how few love to follow Thee to the death of the cross! Willingly will they accompany Thee to Mount Tabor, but they refuse to follow Thee to Calvary. O love, Thou art not loved!

The Month of St. Joseph

PRAYER

O Jesus, infinite goodness, who hast loved man so much and hast done so much to be loved in return, how comes it that Thou art loved so little? I, at least, will not be of this ungrateful number; I desire to love Thee with all my heart and to my last breath. Grant me this grace through the intercession of Thy Foster-father, St. Joseph.

EXAMPLE

A young man who dreaded a military life, was according to the laws of France, obliged to present himself to draw lots for the conscription. On his way to the office he stopped at a little chapel dedicated to St. Joseph-of-the-fields near Laval. Entering in he knelt down and addressing St. Joseph, said: "You know, O Holy Joseph, how greatly I fear a military life, not for the hardships or for the dangers of war, but on account of the idleness and immorality of a barrack life." Then placing a number on the Altar he said, "This is the number I wish to gain; help me."

The Month of St. Joseph

On reaching the office where the lots were drawn, before putting his hand in the box he again invoked St. Joseph. His prayer was heard, he drew the very number he had asked for and which exempted him from military service. With his heart overflowing with joy and gratitude he returned to St. Joseph's Chapel to thank him for the signal favor he had obtained.

FIFTEENTH DAY

ST. JOSEPH THE MODEL OF FAMILY LIFE

I. What is prejudicial in family life.
II. What is exemplary in family life.

First Point.—One of the great evils of the present day is the want of family union. A spirit of independence is rampant and is fast weakening the most sacred family ties. A want of the judicious exercise of authority in parents, the disinclination of children to obey, the love of liberty and independence, these are among the causes of family disunion. One of the most efficacious means of correcting this evil is devotion to St. Joseph, the head and model of the Holy Family at Nazareth. Contemplate this illustrious patriarch, whose humble dwelling is dearer to him than a royal palace. Foster-father of the divine Child he is at once his master and his instructor; he teaches Him his trade, and shows Him how to handle his tools, and Jesus takes pleasure in His father's lessons. He was a carpenter and the Son of a carpenter. *Faber et fabri filius*, this was the title He gloried in.

Parents, learn from St. Joseph's example to maintain authority over your children, and bring them up industriously, so that they may be a comfort and support to you in your old age. And you, children, be considerate to your parents; treat them with respect, and never omit to render them any little service in your power. Above all, pray earnestly to God to direct you in your choice of a state of life.

Second Point—What helps to maintain a spirit of family union, is the faithful observance of religious duties. Where it is possible all should unite in morning and evening prayer; attendance at Mass on the Sunday and festival days must never be omitted. Let Jesus, Mary, and Joseph be our models, for they always went to the Temple at the stated times. "I have seen many instances," said a pious author, "of the visible protection of St. Joseph in those families where he has been especially honored and invoked, such as conversions, miraculous cures, and temporal blessings, too many to enumerate. Let us then often invoke with confidence this great saint; for, if families did but take him for their patron, they would be much more united."

PRAYER

O blessed Joseph, when I mix with the world I feel myself less recollected and less disposed to fulfil the duties of my state of life; obtain grace for me to love retirement and domestic life. Bless my parents, and above all, bless my home, so that it may be as a sanctuary in which I can serve God and fulfil the duties of my state of life. Amen.

EXAMPLE

We read in the life of the Venerable Mother Mary of the Incarnation the following incident. Madame de la Peltrie, who was a Frenchwoman of eminent virtue, happened one day to read an account of a mission which the Fathers of the Society of

The Month of St. Joseph

Jesus had undertaken in Canada. The history of this mission made an impression upon her and she felt a great wish to cooperate in the conversion of the poor Canadians. Before she could make up her mind as to the best means of assisting in the work, she was seized with a severe and alarming illness which baffled the skill of the physicians, who were convinced she could never recover. In the midst of her sufferings Madame de la Peltrie did not forget her pious intention, and God inspired her to make a vow to St. Joseph, under whose powerful protection the Jesuit missioners had placed the conversion of Canada, that if she recovered she would found and endow a convent in Canada for the education of girls. No sooner had the invalid pronounced her vow than her prayer was heard. The violent pains which had caused her such agony left her instantaneously, and nothing remained but a slight weakness. When the physician returned the next day he was astonished at the change, for which he could in no way account.

"Madame," he exclaimed, "what has become of your excruciating pains; where are they gone?"

The Month of St. Joseph

"Why, my dear sir," she replied, smiling, "I believe they are gone to Canada."

She soon after fulfilled her vow, and built the convent she had promised for the education of the young Canadians, and Mother Mary of the Incarnation, so justly esteemed and destined by God for the foreign missions, was its first superior. It was revealed to her in a vision, that St. Joseph was the Patron of the New World, and that is was through his intercession she had been called to labor there for the salvation of souls. She gave the new convent the name of the "Seminary of St. Joseph," and adopted as its seal the image of the venerable Patriarch with the Infant Savior in his arms.

SIXTEENTH DAY

ST. JOSEPH OUR MODEL FOR RECOLLECTION

I. Presence of God.
II. Presence of Jesus Christ.

First Point.—It is not difficult to believe that St. Joseph kept himself habitually in the presence of God, and on this account he was frequently favored with heavenly communications. *Arcanorum celestium secretarius.* In a special manner the mysteries of the Incarnation and of the Redemption were made known to him, *Particeps mysteriorum.* Often had he the privilege of conversing with the angels, and he was favored with such numerous instances of God's providence and Holy Presence, the recollections of which filled his mind and heart so entirely that even his daily labor

The Month of St. Joseph

caused him no distractions. In all things, and in every circumstance, he saw, adored, and blessed God. In his long and painful journeys, in the midst of his laborious employments, never did he lose sight of this adorable presence, which enabled him to follow the inspirations of grace, and accomplish in all things the designs of Providence. We can then apply to the Head of the Holy Family the same words that in Genesis were spoken of the first Joseph: "The Lord was with him, and made all that he did prosper" (Gen. 39:23).

Consider, Christian soul, that the realization of the presence of God has always been regarded in all conditions of life as the great source of perfection: "Walk before me," said the Lord to Abraham, "and be perfect" (Gen. xvii. 1). The very thought that God sees us, sees all our actions, sees all our trials, that He keeps an account of all, and of every desire, of even a simple wish, of which He is the object, this thought is sufficient to inspire us with courage, and enable us to accept every sacrifice. Let us then ask God, through the intercession of St. Joseph, that we may always realize His presence, but chiefly when we begin our prayers and our most important actions.

Second Point.—It was not only the habitual thought of the Presence of God that regulated the life and actions of St. Joseph; God Himself was present before him in the person of Jesus Christ. Most truly might he exclaim with St. John: "We saw His glory, the glory, as it were, of the only-begotten of the Father, full of grace and truth" (John, I. 14). After the Blessed Virgin, St. Joseph had been the first human being to see Him. Thirty years of his life had been spent with Jesus; he lived with Him under the same roof; he shared his meals with Him; he watched Him at His work, and when in prayer; he gathered lessons from all His actions, and edification from His example; in a word, he was always with Jesus. Sleep even did not interrupt this union; for, said a pious author, if his eyes were closed his heart watched; and if, for a short time, he was deprived of the corporal presence of the Savior, His image was ever present to his mind and heart. It is not surprising that in the sacred Presence our Holy Patron should advance rapidly in the paths of perfection, and rising above all created sanctity, that after Jesus and Mary he should shine as the most brilliant star in the

The Month of St. Joseph

heavenly firmament.

The real presence of Jesus, which during thirty years formed St. Joseph's joy, can, O Christian soul, form your happiness also. In the Eucharist we have Jesus in the midst of us, and at any hour of the day we can visit and converse with Him. But do we do so? Do we in this respect imitate St. Joseph? Oh, let us arouse our faith, and let us often visit the Divine Emmanuel. He is the same in the tabernacle as He was in His mortal life, the refuge of sinners, the friend of the righteous, the consoler of the afflicted, the Savior of souls.

PRAYER

O holy Joseph, I desire to live henceforth like thee in the presence of God, and more especially in the presence of Jesus in the Eucharist. whom I resolve to visit often in the Sacrament of His love. The remembrance of it will cause me to be more recollected. Obtain the grace for me, O great Saint, to be faithful to my resolution. Amen.

The Month of St. Joseph

EXAMPLE

The following interesting fact, which is related in the "History of the Order of Reformed Carmelites," as having occurred to Brother John the Evangelist of the same order, may serve to illustrate the zeal and charity of St. Joseph in assisting those who are devoted to him.

"I was going," said the Brother, "from the convent of the Carmelite Nuns of the Pilastro del Toro, accompanied by Brother Peter of the Incarnation, who was procurator of the Convent of the Holy Martyrs of Granada, when we met a man about fifty years of age, of pleasing countenance; his appearance was noble and venerable, and he was attired in black. He placed himself between us and asked whence we came? My companion answered, that we had just left the Convent of the Discalced Carmelite Nuns.

"Father," said the stranger, "can you tell me why your order is so devoted to St. Joseph?"

The Religious replied, "Because our holy Mother Teresa of Jesus so greatly honored that glorious Saint, who most wonderfully

The Month of St. Joseph

assisted her in the foundation of her convents, and obtained for her from Heaven so many special graces, that through gratitude to him she dedicated the greater number of the convents she founded to his honor,"

"I am aware of that," said the stranger. "Look at me, and learn from her example to honor him as much as she did. Whatsoever you shall ask through his intercession you shall most certainly obtain."

Having said this he disappeared, and on looking round we saw no one. On returning to our convent, where the blessed Father John of the Cross was Prior, we related to him what had happened.

"The stranger," he said, "was no other than St. Joseph; it was for me more than for you this apparition was intended, as I have not honored this great Saint as much as I should have done; but I will endeavor to profit by the favor conferred on you." This occurred in the year 1584.

SEVENTEENTH DAY

ST. JOSEPH, MODEL OF OBEDIENCE

I. Entire Obedience.
II. Prompt Obedience.

First Point.—"Obedience alone," said St. Augustine, "is worth more than all other virtues;" *Plus valet quam omnes virtutes,* and in the eyes of God it is worth more than sacrifice. The life of St. Joseph was a constant practice of this great virtue. Scripture tells us that Joseph obeyed the potentates of the world; for it was to conform to Cesar's edict that he went with Mary his spouse to Nazareth to be enrolled. Joseph obeyed the angels. When in doubt as to whether he should part from Mary, the angel told him to remain, and he did so. Joseph obeyed God. All that the Law prescribed he did it at the time, in the manner, and in the place prescribed by the Law. Three times a year did

The Month of St. Joseph

he go to Jerusalem for the celebration of the festivals. At the time prescribed by the law he took the Infant Jesus to be circumcised, and with Mary presented Him in the Temple. St. Joseph's obedience was entire, it extended to everything. "How admirable," said St. Francis of Sales, "was the obedience of our holy Patriarch. See how perfectly on every occasion he was submissive to the decrees of Heaven."

Is your obedience, O Christian soul, entire and universal, like that of your glorious model? Do you obey all the laws of God and the Church, without exception and without reserve? Is there not some precept that you neglect entirely? St. James says, "whosoever shall keep the whole law, but offend in one point, is become guilty of all" (James 2:10). Happy indeed is he, O holy Joseph, who, following your example, makes the law of God the rule of his conduct; he will, like you, find therein a source of true happiness. *Qui custodit legem beatus est.*

Second Point.—The second characteristic of Joseph's obedience was its prompitude. If we consider it in the most serious and painful circumstances of his life, we shall everywhere find that he obeyed generously, without delay, and without a murmur. A celebrated author compares his soul to molten metal ready to take whatever form God willed to give it. When required to lay aside his work at Nazareth and undertake a long journey in the cold winter season, in order to conform to the orders of Augustus Cæsar, he delayed not but set out immediately with Mary. Did he procrastinate when the angel bade him "arise and take the Child and His Mother, and fly into Egypt," to escape from Herod's fury? No, he rose before the break of day, and without making any preparations, fled into Egypt. Did he refuse to return to the land of Israel, when the angel announced that Herod was dead, and bade the Holy Family return? No, he arose and set out with the Child and his Mother, notwithstanding his fear of Archelaus, the cruel son of Herod. How many difficulties would not others have raised, but not so Joseph; without a moment's hesitation he obeyed like the angels, cheerfully and with alacrity. His only answer was, "Lord, behold me ready."

Christian soul, remember that hesitation in obedience implies resistance. To put off obeying as long as possible, and not to obey till after many explanations, is not a voluntary but a forced act of obedience; it is like a faded flower which has lost its freshness and perfume. How can such an act be pleasing in God's sight?

PRAYER

O my loving and holy protector, accomplished model of perfect obedience, obtain the grace for me to understand the necessity and advantages of this precious virtue. Teach me to obey with promptitude and joy, for the love of Jesus, as thou didst. Amen.

EXAMPLE

Father Joseph Lambillotte, a celebrated musician, was known like his two brothers Louis and Francis, not only for his musical talents, but for his abilities in the education of youth. The good Father was remarkable also for his filial devotion to his patron, St. Joseph. Owing to the feeble state of his

The Month of St. Joseph

health he was obliged to relinquish teaching, and the last three years of his life were passed at St. Acheul, suffering from consumption. In the leisure moments this illness afforded him, he composed the book entitled "The Consoler," a work full of feeling, and which has been of much service to a great many souls.

In the month of March, 1842, a very serious crisis occurred which alarmed every one. Let us pray much for Father Lambillotte, said the Novice Master, for he is in a very dangerous state; all the same I do not think he will die, for he has asked St. Joseph not to let him die until he had finished writing his book. Before very long the good Father was sufficiently recovered to continue his work, and a Novice was appointed to help him by writing from his dictation. One day he announced that his book was finished; it was then August, and on the 12th the last sheet was placed in the printer's hands. On the 14th the good Father breathed his last. It was the vigil of the Assumption, and all hoped he would contemplate the next day in Heaven the Immaculate Spouse of his powerful Advocate.

EIGHTEENTH DAY

ST. JOSEPH, MODEL OF VIRGINAL CHASTITY

I. The perfection of chastity.
II. The reward of chastity.

First Point.—The most pure of all creatures is Mary, and next to her St. Joseph ranks as the most chaste of men. His name, like the name of the Queen of Angels, bespeaks virginity. According to St. Thomas, God had bestowed on St. Joseph graces that sanctified him before his birth, extinguished the fire of concupiscence and made him as an angel, though clothed in flesh. St. Jerome and several of the Fathers of the Church are of the opinion, that like Mary he made a vow of virginity in the early years of his life, and how could the purity of Joseph but increase when he was constituted the Guardian and Protector of Mary's virginity! The Immaculate Queen was the resplendent mirror of the sun of justice, whose rays reflected on her chaste spouse. "He was angelic and virginal in all things," said St. Teresa, "and for that reason angels were sent to reveal to him the secrets of Heaven."

Purity is the most beautiful of all virtues, for it raises man by making him participate as it were in the nature of angels, or rather, it may be said, it raises human nature above the angels; for they know not the allurements of pleasure nor the seductions of the senses; whereas purity makes us live the lives of angels, notwithstanding the corruption and weakness of our flesh. "Blessed are the clean of heart" (Matt. 5:8). Holy Joseph, obtain this angelic virtue for me, and remove from me all that may endanger it. In order to preserve it I will watch, pray, and be devout to thee.

Second Point.—Joseph's virginity was admirably rewarded. It was because he was the most pure of men that he merited to become the Spouse of Mary; "For," says St. Jerome, "if the Virgin Mary was to be given after the death of Christ to the care of a disciple who was a virgin, by how much greater reason was she to be confided to the care of a virgin spouse." In the words of

Bossuet, "their Espousals could be but the union of two virginal hearts, virginal then and always in their chastity." Nor was this St. Joseph's only privilege; for it was his virginity that caused him to be chosen as the Foster-father of our Lord. Yes, Jesus whose delight is to be in the midst of lilies, was pleased to call the holy Patriarch by the sweet name of Father, to rest in his arms, and to pass thirty years of His life under the shadow of this beautiful lily. *Pascitur inter lilia.* Blessed then was the virginity of Joseph, which permitted him to say to the Son of the Eternal Father, "Thou art my Son," and to the Mother of God, "Thou art my Spouse. *Virginitate placuit.*"

If you follow Joseph's example, Christian soul, and practice purity, Jesus and Mary will favor you as they did him. In the Canticle of Canticles the chaste soul receives the title of the Sister, the friend, the spouse of the Son of God, who delights in her conversation and in the sound of her voice, who loves to have her with Him and for whom He reserves a special reward in the Kingdom of Heaven. This holy virtue spiritualizes our human nature even before the resurrection; the flesh is conquered, and becomes as it were angelic,

The Month of St. Joseph

Angelica caro, and even in this world its conquest is one of the elements of our greatness; oh! how blessed and beautiful are pure souls.

PRAYER

I understand now, O St. Joseph, why thou art represented with a lily in thy band; this white flower is a symbol of thy inviolable purity. Touch me with this pure lily, which exhales the perfume of virginity, and divine love will then be enkindled within me, and after having imitated the holiness of thy heart on earth, it will be given me to possess the God of all purity with thee forever in Heaven. Amen.

EXAMPLE

A pious young man was studying for the Church with the Parish Priest of the village in which he unfortunately, he experienced such difficulty in learning Latin, that his teacher losing all patience was inclined to give up instructing him. The youth, however, redoubled his efforts; and a longer trial was allowed him. "My good boy," said the old Priest one day, "I see but one way out of the difficulty, and that is for you to put yourself under the protection of St. Joseph, and to pray and beseech him to obtain for you the talents that are wanting in you; otherwise you will never make any progress. Come, have a little courage; I will join my prayers to yours, and I feel confident our prayers will be heard; for perseverance in prayer obtains everything." The youth followed the advice given and prayed so fervently that the results proved his petition had been granted. His mind seemed to open little by little and his talents to develop in a wonderful manner, so that he finished the course of his studies successfully, and entered the Seminary, where he was distinguished not only for virtue but for talent; and after a time taking honors he was ordained Priest. In later years he was named Professor of moral and dogmatic Theology, and finally was appointed Vicar-General, which post he occupied for many years, proving himself to be a prudent and enlightened Director of the clergy. But the one thing for which he was remarkable was his unbounded confidence in

The Month of St. Joseph

St. Joseph and his gratitude to his generous protector. Let us learn from this example the power with God of humble and persevering prayer, when addressed to Him through the intercession of the Holy Spouse of Mary.

NINETEENTH DAY

THE FEAST OF ST. JOSEPH

I. It ought to give joy.
II. It ought to inspire confidence.

First Point.—The Feast of St. Joseph was kept as a double of the second class, as were the feasts of the Apostles, until the year 1870, when Pius IX conferred upon the holy Patriarch the title of Patron of the Universal Church, and raised his feast to the same rank as the great solemnities of our Lord and the Blessed Virgin. Let us rejoice that the Vicar of Christ should have given this fresh mark of honor to the head of the Holy Family. All that tends to the glory of a Father reflects on his children and becomes an occasion of rejoicing to them; shall not we then be glad and rejoice that the 19th of March will in future be a day dear to us and to all pious

The Month of St. Joseph

clients of St. Joseph; it is the day that the Lord has made: *Hæc dies quam fecit Dominus.* O great St. Teresa, you who wished to see others animated with the feelings of devotion and veneration with which you were animated for St. Joseph, rejoice now, your wishes are beginning to be fulfilled. Love for him reigns in every heart which loves our Lord; St. Joseph's praises are on every Catholic lip and millions of voices join the choirs of angels in celebrating his festival on earth.

Christian soul, on this solemn festival day withdraw from the turmoil of life and live in spirit with the Holy Family, where all breathes of Heaven and holy love. It is not one incident only of St. Joseph's life that you should contemplate on this great day; recall all his virtues and thank God for having given you such a tender Father, such a powerful protector, such a perfect model.

May all created beings bless Thee, O Lord, for all that Thou hast done for St. Joseph.

Second Point.—But not with joy only should our hearts be filled, we should also feel great confidence; for if we can rely on the powerful protection of St. Joseph every day of the year, how much more may we not hope to receive from him on this auspicious day, a day which sees the Universal Church prostrate at his feet, and on which the Son of God places in the hands of His Foster-father his choicest gifts to bestow upon us. If worldly potentates grant favors on days of public rejoicings, what favors may we not hope for from the most merciful of the saints, from Joseph, the Foster-father of Jesus, the Spouse of Mary, the protector of the Catholic Church; from Joseph who has been appointed by God Himself to minister to our wants. Let us listen to what St. Teresa says:

"I cannot remember during many years having asked him on St. Joseph's feast day any favor that I did not receive; and if there was anything injurious or imperfect in my petition he rectified it for my greater good." The same happy results will be experienced by those who invoke St. Joseph with confidence and are faithful in keeping his feast.

Let us then with great confidence have recourse to the Spouse of Mary, let us ask him to obtain for us the spiritual and temporal graces that we need. Let us recommend to him our families, our benefactors, our friends, and our relatives living and dead. Let us pray for the Pope and the Church, let us pray especially for a happy death; and what more fitting day can we have to ask for this greatest of graces but this very day when the whole Church recalls the moment of St. Joseph's happy passage from time to eternity, when she celebrates the day that was for him the commencement of a life of glory, the just recompense of his virtues.

PRAYER

O glorious Saint, whose festival the Church celebrates this day, and whose praises are chanted in heaven, I join fervently in this solemn Hosanna which is raised in thy honor. Since thou wilt not refuse anything to thy servants on this joyful day, obtain all the graces that are necessary for me, I beseech thee; but above all obtain for me the inestimable grace of loving Jesus and Mary as thou didst, and of dying in their arms.

The Month of St. Joseph

EXAMPLE

A Father of the Society of Jesus came to Viré in France, in the beginning of the Lent of 1854, to preach a Mission there, but, owing to unforeseen circumstances, the three Fathers who were to have assisted him in this important work were prevented coming. Viré contained about 10,000 inhabitants, and there was every prospect of the mission being productive of great good; but now how was this possible; a single priest was not sufficient for such a harvest. The Father wrote to his superiors and implored help, but it was all in vain; no help could be given. The Feast of St. Joseph was at hand, and on the eve, when preparing for his meditation, the Father met with these words of St. Teresa: "I never remember to have asked St. Joseph for anything without having obtained it, and for many years I have asked some particular grace on his feast and have never failed to be heard."

The next day, as soon as his meditation was finished, he wrote three letters, and giving them to the priest, said: "Our Mission will be given; here are three letters which I place under the protection of St. Joseph, I

The Month of St. Joseph

have asked him for Missioners and he will come to our assistance. St. Teresa says she never failed to obtain of this great Saint what she asked on his feast." The clergy and people of Viré, though they had wished much for a Mission, had now given up all hopes, and laughingly said to the Father:

"You have moved heaven and earth in vain; do you still hope? All the saints in heaven have failed you, and do you think St. Joseph will grant your request, and that he has Missioners ready to set out at his pleasure?" The obstacles were certainly great, but divine Providence willed to glorify St. Joseph and show how powerful was his intercession. A few days passed, when, at the moment he was least expected, a Father arrived from Belgium; next day two other Fathers came, sent from the Jesuits' house at Angers. Each letter had brought a Father, and one of them had to leave a work of importance which he could not make up his mind to do until he had prayed to St. Joseph to direct him. The favor obtained so unexpectedly becoming known, the people flocked to the Mission which was given with the happiest results.

TWENTIETH DAY

JOSEPH THE MODEL OF PRAYER

I. Of Vocal Prayer.
II. Of Mental Prayer.

First Point.—St. Joseph was a perfect model of vocal prayer; for he understood its importance and its advantages. We may safely then believe that with this holy exercise he began and sanctified his days, his actions, and his journeys, and that he prayed with great recollection and angelic fervor.

Christian soul, follow the precept of the Divine Master and pray always. If you are able, establish the pious practice of prayers in common, at least as regards night prayer; for great are the advantages of this holy custom. The recollection of family night prayers has often left an impression on the minds of children that after-years could not efface, and blessings have attended parents who have kept up the custom. Our Lord said: "Where there are two or three gathered together in my name there am I in the midst of them; and whatsoever they ask, it shall be done to them by my Father who is in heaven (Matt. 18:19, 20). How consoling is this promise! O Jesus, O Joseph, teach us how to pray.

Second Point.—St. Joseph is rightly honored as the father and model of contemplative souls. St. Bernardine of Siena says that he had received the gift of prayer in a very high degree. *Fuit altissimus in contemplatione.* St. Teresa relates that she always noticed that those who prayed to St. Joseph with confidence made rapid progress in mental prayer, and the Church invokes him as a Master of contemplation. St. Joseph's heart being so habitually absorbed in God, his life was a continual prayer; and as his soul received thus daily increase of virtue it produced abundant fruits for eternal life.

Christian soul, resolve to make a meditation every day, if but for a short time; for it is a most efficacious means of salvation. "Make me a promise," said St. Teresa, "to make a quarter of an hour's meditation every day, and in the name of Jesus Christ I promise you heaven." Those on the contrary who neglect this holy exercise, will not need the devil to drag them to hell; they drag themselves there. Does not the Holy Ghost say: "With desolation is all the land made desolate, because there is none that considereth in the heart" (Jer. 12:11). Obtain for me the grace, O holy Joseph, to imitate thee in thy love of prayer, and thy fidelity in practicing it.

PRAYER

Permit me to unite myself at this moment, O St. Joseph, to the prayer that thou didst offer with Jesus and Mary at Nazareth. Grant that I may pray like thee with faith, humility, and perseverance. Grant that I may pray in union with Jesus and Mary. Amen.

EXAMPLE

In the monastery of St. Elizabeth, at Lyons, a religious named Margaret Rigaud, met with a dangerous fall which rendered her insensible, and caused the blood to issue from her mouth, nose, and ears. By means of strong remedies and great care her life was preserved, but her head was so weakened that for several months she could not bear to lean it on the pillow, and her mental faculties were so impaired that she found it impossible to apply herself to anything. The physicians and surgeons, after holding a consultation, agreed that her only chance of recovery was to submit to the operation of trepanning. This decision caused the poor patient so great a shock that the doctors thought it advisable to defer the operation for a few days. In the meantime the Superior determined to try a more easy and effectual course, and ordered all the sisters to make a Novena of Communions in honor of St. Joseph. The pains continued as violent as ever, and at length towards the end of the Novena some of the sisters, despairing of obtaining their request through the intercession of St. Joseph, thought it would be better to substitute St. Anselm, to whose protection they usually had recourse in cases of accidents. But one of the sisters, who greatly venerated and loved St. Joseph, redoubled her entreaties, and begged him to effect the cure himself, representing that it

The Month of St. Joseph

would be quite derogatory to his honor, which they were so desirous to promote, if he yielded the glory of such a miracle to any other saint, and promised that if restored to health the invalid should herself make a novena of acts of mortifications, devotions, and thanksgiving. Whilst the pious sister persevered in prayer without intermission, the invalid was perfectly cured, and at a moment when least expected. She happened to be alone, and dressing quickly she ran about the monastery unable to control her joy, calling out, "a miracle, a miracle, St. Joseph has cured me." What followed proved that her cure was complete; for the same day she assisted in choir and recited office with the other sisters, though previously she had not been able to bear even the distant sound of their voices; she also resumed her usual occupations with an energy which surprised everyone. In a word, St. Joseph, obtained for her not only the restoration of her health, but many other favors which greatly contributed to her spiritual advancement.

TWENTY-FIRST DAY

ST. JOSEPH, MODEL OF POVERTY

I. He suffered all the bitterness of poverty.
II. He tasted all the consolations.

First Point.—Though Joseph was a descendant of the Kings of Juda, his family had become impoverished, so that, in the words of Bossuet, his inheritance was no other than his hands, and no resource was his beyond that of labor. In order to procure a livelihood he learnt to be a carpenter. His union with Mary did not place him in a better position, for her ancestors had also fallen into poverty. In the humble dwelling of Nazareth everything spoke of poverty; the scanty furniture, the linen, the clothing, all was simple and coarse. After the birth of Jesus Joseph's poverty increased. Bossuet speaks of it in these words: "Joseph and Mary were poor, but they had not yet suffered from the

The Month of St. Joseph

want of a roof to shelter them. "But when the Infant God came into the world no house could they find, owing to their poverty, and a stable was the only shelter they could procure."

The poverty of Joseph was indeed great, exclaimed St. Francis of Sales; he was often in need of the necessaries of life for the support of his family, and this must have been a great trial to his paternal heart; nevertheless he bore lovingly these cruel privations, which were not momentary, but lasted all his life, and he humbly submitted to this long trial of poverty.

O you, to whom God has refused the riches of this world, be comforted; He treats you as He treats those he loves, as He treated St. Joseph, his representative on earth, as He treated Jesus his own Son. When you are tempted to complain of the privation of fortune, enter in spirit into the stable of Bethlehem, and into the house of Nazareth, and at the sight of this example of evangelical poverty, say to yourself, am I worthy of a better lot than that of Jesus, Mary, and Joseph?

The Month of St. Joseph

Second Point.—Jesus, who by embracing poverty, condemned the inordinate love of riches, had imbued St. Joseph with a contempt for the goods of this life and a love of poverty. Often reduced to extreme penury, obliged to gain his livelihood and that of the Holy Family by the sweat of his brow, in his humble work shop, the holy patriarch enjoyed a happiness unknown to those who dwell in sumptuous palaces. In possessing nothing he possessed everything; and was he not truly rich in the possession of Jesus and Mary? The words of the first Beatitude may be applied to Joseph. You are happy in poverty for the kingdom of heaven is yours.

Christian soul, do you wish to taste the consolations that God attaches to poverty, love the poor, and relieve them. Happy is he who understands the mystery of poverty, and helps the poor. The man who is compassionate benefits himself, and will not fall into indigence. With what confidence will not those appear before God who have loved and helped the poor.

The Month of St. Joseph

PRAYER

Great Saint, thou who wast truly poor in mind and heart, and who didst share the poverty of Jesus, obtain for thy servants an esteem and love for the treasure whose price thou didst so well know. Grant also that they may understand that loving and relieving the poor is a source of blessings, and a pledge of salvation. Amen.

EXAMPLE

A zealous old priest, who for many years had the care of the homes in Paris for destitute youths, found it necessary to build a new chapel, as the old one could no longer accommodate the boys. The building was begun at the estimated cost of about 80,000 francs, and by the time it was completed the good priest had managed by dint of much labor and patience to collect the greater part of the money. There was still, however, three thousand francs owing. and the contractor threatened to take law proceedings unless these were paid in a fortnight. The poor old

The Month of St. Joseph

priest, frightened at the threat, threw himself on his knees before the statue of St. Joseph, and besought him to come to his assistance, commencing a novena at the same time for that object.

The days passed on but no one brought him a franc. On the last day of the novena, whilst kneeling at the feet of the statue, he was told some one was waiting to speak to him. It was a servant girl, who, giving the number and name of a street, said a lady living there wished to see him. The priest, supposing it to be a sick call, went at once, and found a lady who, far from looking an invalid, was the picture of health.

After the usual greetings, she said, "I have just come into a considerable amount of property, and wishing to show my gratitude to God by an act of charity, I made inquiries, and heard of you and the chapel you were building; do me the pleasure to accept this as your share of my good fortune"; and so saying she handed him three bank-notes of a thousand francs each. It was the exact sum the good priest needed for the debt to the contractor, and for which he had prayed to St. Joseph with such fervor and with such confidence.

> # TWENTY-SECOND DAY

ST. JOSEPH OUR MODEL IN SUFFERING

I. His exterior suffering.
II. His interior suffering.

First Point.—According to the teaching of St. Paul, just souls have to suffer. "All that will live godly in Christ Jesus shall suffer persecution" (2 Tim. 3:12). We must acknowledge that after Mary, St. Joseph has been the most tried of all the mints. Contemplate him in the various circumstances of his life at Nazareth, at Bethlehem, and in Egypt; and you will see that during his whole life he had everywhere to suffer poverty; and not only did he suffer from poverty, but he suffered from the inclemency of the seasons, from the

The Month of St. Joseph

hardships of a long and painful exile, and from the contempt, the injustice, and ingratitude of men. Jesus, who loved him tenderly as His Foster-father, made him drink of the chalice of His sufferings during life, in order that he might share in the great mystery of the Redemption. St. Joseph was then the first and most faithful disciple of the Cross, the first confessor, and we may almost say, the first martyr of Jesus Christ.

The Cross has always been and always will be the royal standard of the elect. Suffering souls, take courage; Jesus goes before you, Mary and Joseph will help you, the Saints entreat you to advance, the Angels register your struggles and your victories. Heaven counts the wound you receive. Take courage then, a few more steps on the path of sorrow, a few more acts of love, a few more bitter tears shed in union with Mary, a little oftener a fiat with Jesus in the garden agony, and Heaven is yours. *Si compatimur, ita et conglorificemen.* O Joseph, obtain for me the grace that I may learn to sow with you in tears, so that one day I may reap in joy.

Second Point.—Great as were the bodily sufferings of St. Joseph, yet the sufferings of

The Month of St. Joseph

his mind and heart were still greater. He understood the Prophecy of Holy Simeon concerning Jesus; he knew that his adopted Son would be put to death for the redemption of mankind; and this thought was as a sword of grief which pierced his heart; truly was this a daily and hourly martyrdom that love only enabled him to bear. How many tears did the holy Patriarch shed at the thought of Mary at the foot of the cross upon which Jesus was crucified, and which cross was ever present to his mind. "Often," wrote a pious author, "did he experience sadness like to death, and he could not have borne it had not the Divine Child supported and strengthened him by a secret strength which passed from His heart. What agony, O sinners, have not your sins caused Mary and Joseph.

Christian soul, you suffer also from interior pains, secret and heart-rending pains that the world neither sees nor understands, and is powerless to relieve. But come to Joseph, open your heart to him, and weep at the feet of your holy Patron, of him who has had so large a share of sufferings. He will feel for you, and help to dry your tears. *Adjutor in tempore tribulationis.*

The Month of St. Joseph

PRAYER

Thou didst suffer, O Holy Joseph, notwithstanding that thy life was so innocent; and I, though I have sinned, have no wish to suffer; thou didst suffer with peace and submission, whilst I am impatient under the slightest trial. O admirable model of resignation, I beseech thee to obtain for me grace to bear patiently all the trials that may be sent me. Amen.

EXAMPLE

The following remarkable revelation regarding the value of suffering, is worthy of being narrated; it was made by St. Joseph to the Venerable Maria d'Escobar. This servant of God being in an ecstasy on the 19th of March, 1627, had a vision of the holy Patriarch, who appeared to her in great glory, and attended by myriads of angels. His countenance though majestic beamed with paternal kindness.

"He approached," these are her own words, "and having graciously saluted me,

The Month of St. Joseph

said: 'The Lord be with thee, I am Joseph, the Spouse of Mary, and am sent by God to visit and console thee.' Having drawn aside the mantle which he wore, I beheld on his breast a brilliant cross about a foot in length, from which issued forth the most resplendent rays. This cross was of such exquisite beauty that I could not but gaze upon it with delight. The saint then spoke to me thus: 'My child, this cross, the sight of which so enraptures thy soul, constituted my happiness whilst on earth. It was my treasure—I gloried in it; I esteemed the grace of suffering then, as I now do, of far greater value in the sight of God than even the immense privilege of having been chosen Spouse of the Blessed Virgin Mary and Foster-father of Jesus. The afflictions with which God has visited thee have, I admit, been very great, and the sufferings which are to be thy portion for the remainder of thy life may surpass in intensity the torments of the martyrs who shed their blood for Christ. Learn to appreciate this favor and to thank God as he deserves for His special predilection in thy regard. The cross is of infinite value, and shines with rare splendor in Heaven; it is the distinctive mark of those chosen souls upon whom God has conferred the grace of resembling His Only Son Jesus Christ. If thou be faithful in corresponding with this grace, God will raise thee to a high degree of glory in the next life. Be consoled then, my child; for the pains and sufferings of this life are transitory, but the crown of glory and the possession of God are eternal." Having spoken thus, the holy Patriarch, perceiving that his client still remained in admiration of the cross suspended on his breast, presented it for her to kiss; after which he gave her his blessing by placing his hand upon her head and forehead, and disappeared, leaving her filled with excessive joy."

TWENTY-THIRD DAY

ST. JOSEPH, MODEL OF LABOR

I. He labored for Jesus and Mary.
II. He labored with Jesus and Mary.

First Point.—Having neither fortune nor position St. Joseph was obliged to do hard and constant work in order to provide food for the Holy Family; he was a carpenter, and in the early Christian ages the yokes and ploughs which were the work of his hands were preserved as precious relics. Let us contemplate this holy Patriarch, this scion of the Kings of Juda, this son of David, working from early dawn until nightfall for the Incarnate Word and for the Queen of Heaven. His mission might seem insignificant in the eyes of men, but it was great in God's sight; men judge only by what they see, but God sees the heart. Blessed are the hands, O Jesus, that provided for Thy earthly needs and those of Thy Holy Mother, at the cost of such long and painful labor.

You, whose lot it is to toil, never forget the lessons that Nazareth teaches, and remember that however humble may be your employment, the laborer is an honor to his family. With the example of Jesus and Joseph, who had to live by the work of their hands and the sweat of their brows, no state of life is more honorable than that of a Christian workman.

Second Point.—After considering how Joseph labored for Jesus and Mary, we must now contemplate him working with Jesus and Mary. In his humble workshop, the holy Patriarch gave the first lessons in labor to the child Jesus, who, as He advanced in age helped His Foster-father. St. Liguori says, that we may well believe that St. Joseph's heart was inflamed with love when he saw his Divine Master serve him as would a fellow-laborer, opening and closing the workshop, helping him to saw and carry the wood, in a word, assisting him in all his work. Could Joseph complain of the hardships of his life, when he beheld Jesus sharing his labors, and Mary at work in their humble dwelling.

Christian soul, let us also work with Jesus. Let us do everything for Him, in Him, and with Him. Let us remember that our labors will not avail for eternity if they are not performed with purity of intention. We shall have sown but there will be nothing to reap. If, on the contrary, we work like Joseph, in the presence of Jesus and Mary, our labors will not be without their reward, and each hardship we undergo will be a gem in our Heavenly crown.

PRAYER

Blessed Joseph, thou who wert so little in the eyes of men but so exalted before God, obtain for me the grace to sanctify my toil as thou didst by a spirit of faith, piety, and love. May I perform all my actions in such a way that they may merit an increase of grace in this world and an additional glory in Heaven. Amen.

EXAMPLE

Joseph le Saige de la Villebrune, who was lieutenant in the Pontifical Zouaves, was remarkable for his great devotion to Bt. Joseph, who, in consequence rewarded him visibly on his death-bed. Feeling the near approach of death he sent for the military chaplain, saying: "St. Joseph has ordered me to make my confession immediately, and I know there is not a minute to lose."

After hearing his confession the chaplain said, "I am now going to say Mass for you, after which I will bring you the Holy Viaticum;" but the dying man sent again for him just as he was about beginning Mass, saying, if he waited till it was finished it would be too late, as by that time he would have lost consciousness and should not recover it. He then recited aloud prayers in preparation for Communion, and after receiving, he thanked God for the grace which had been bestowed upon him, and for the warning of approaching death that he had received. The fervor of his devotion edified all who were present. As he had predicted, no sooner had he finished his prayers, than he was seized with a fit of

The Month of St. Joseph

delirium; his eyes were closed, but after awhile opening them he made an effort to rise, and throwing himself at the feet of the statue of St. Joseph, called out to the nurse, "Make haste and bring me my clothes, for St. Joseph is waiting for me; cannot you see he is standing there waiting for me." Next day about three in the morning he raised himself on his bed, opened his eyes and fixing them on the statue, without any agony gently breathed his last.

TWENTY-FOURTH DAY

THE HAPPY DEATH OF JOSEPH

I. He dies assisted by Mary.
II. He dies assisted by Jesus.

First Point.—A life full of grace and merit as had been the life of Joseph could not close otherwise than with a holy and happy death. The time had come when Jesus was to dwell no longer in Nazareth, but was to manifest Himself to the world. Joseph's mission was then ended. After passing thirty years with Jesus and Mary one thing only was wanting to complete his happiness, and that was that he should die in their arms. Full of gratitude for all that Joseph had done for her, Mary redoubled her tender care of him in these his last moments. She watched beside him, administering all that he required with a tender love worthy of the Mother of God. St.

Bernardine of Siena, speaking of the happy death of St. Joseph, assisted by the Queen of Heaven, cannot find words to express what must have been the consolation and love St. Joseph experienced. "O Mary, if in after ages thou hast so often changed the dark shadow of death to the brightness of day for thy faithful servants, what sweetness and consolation must not thy presence have afforded to thy holy and loved spouse in these his last moments.

Do you, Christian soul, like St. Joseph, wish to be assisted and comforted by Mary at your last hour, follow the example of this glorious Patriarch, and during your life love and serve the most Holy Virgin. The remembrance of what we have done in her honor each day will fill our hearts with joy and hope at the hour of death, at that dread moment on which depends our eternity. O Holy Virgin, thou who didst receive the last breath of Joseph, obtain for us from thy Divine Son the grace to die with feelings of true contrition and hope. Yes, O Holy Mother of God, pray for us always, but more especially at the hour of our death.

Second Point.—Let us now contemplate

The Month of St. Joseph

our Lord fulfilling the last filial duties to His Foster-father. We cannot doubt but at this St. Joseph's last hour Jesus rewarded him for all the labors he had undergone by bestowing on him great interior joy, that He rewarded him for the tears he had shed by giving him heavenly consolations, and that He rewarded him for the anguish he had so frequently suffered by giving him peace of soul and a pledge of immortality. It would be at this moment when Jesus watched by the death-bed of the dying Patriarch, that He made him the Protector of the dying and the Patron of a happy death. Scripture speaks not of these last moments, but the words that the Church now makes use of we may piously believe were spoken then, and that Jesus blessing him for the last time uttered the words: "Depart, soul of my Father, and be carried by the angels into Abraham's bosom; the day will soon come when you will ascend to Heaven with me." And the angels obeying their Master's voice, conducted his soul to Limbo where the Patriarchs were awaiting the Redemption.

It depends on ourselves only, O Christian soul, to share m Joseph's happiness. If like him we pass our lives in union with Jesus, He will come and comfort us at our last hour; for death is but the echo of life. O holy Joseph, when I am stretched on my bed of sorrow, tell Jesus to come and visit and bless me. Fortified then with the Holy Viaticum, I shall bid a last farewell to earth, and my soul will wing its flight to Heaven, where with thee I shall contemplate Jesus and Mary for never-ending ages.

PRAYER

O venerated Head of the Holy Family, who after living with Jesus and Mary didst die in their arms, obtain that Jesus and Mary may assist me in my last hour, that the last pulsation of my heart may be an act of love, and their sacred names the last words my dying lips shall utter. Amen.

EXAMPLE

Father Lallemand, who was for some years Rector of the Jesuit College at Bourges, called two of the young professors on the occasion of the Feast of St. Joseph which the

The Month of St. Joseph

students were preparing to celebrate, and promised each of them to obtain some grace that they wished for, on the condition that they would exhort their pupils to be very devout to St. Joseph. The two professors willingly agreed to the proposal, and their exhortations were so effectual, that on the Feast of St. Joseph every student in the two classes received Holy Communion. In the course of the day the two professors went to the Rector's room and told him in private what the grace was that they wished to obtain. The first who spoke was no other than the celebrated Father Nouet, and the grace he asked for was that he might be able to write and speak of our Lord in a manner that would be worthy of Him. The grace which the second professor asked is not known, but he declared that his request had been granted. The day after the Feast, Father Nouet returned to the Rector and told him he had changed his mind, and thought that he ought to ask for a grace that would be of more use in helping him in the path of perfection. The Rector replied that it was too late, for St. Joseph had already obtained the grace he had first asked for.

TWENTY-FIFTH DAY

ST. JOSEPH, PATRON OF A HAPPY DEATH

I. Because he is the Father of our Judge.
II. Because he is the Conqueror of the Devil.

First Point.—"Man knoweth not whether he be worthy of love or hatred" (Eccles. 9:1), and St. Paul expresses the same in these words: "For I am not conscious to myself of anything, yet I am not hereby justified, but He that judgeth me is the Lord" (1 Cor. 4:4). Can these words be read without a thrill of fear? Even persons who lead good lives tremble at the thought of death and judgment, that terrible moment on which depends eternity. *O momentum a quo pendet æternitas.*

But those should feel confidence who are numbered amongst the faithful servants of St. Joseph. From time immemorial this great

The Month of St. Joseph

Saint has been invoked by the Church as the Patron of a happy death. The title he bore on earth of Father to the Sovereign Judge, on whom our eternity will depend, has naturally inspired this devotion. Moses was the chief and guide of the Children of Israel, and yet in his intercourse with God he acted so authoritatively that when he prayed for his rebellious people his prayer became a command which stayed the hand of the Almighty, preventing Him from chastising the guilty ones until Moses as it were permitted it. But with how much more authority will not our holy Patriarch stay the hand of our Sovereign Judge, he whose sublime mission it was when on earth to be the Guide, the Guardian, the Father of Him who will judge the living and the dead! Yes, at that dread hour St. Joseph will be our intercessor with the great Judge before whom we shall have to appear. With such an advocate our eternal salvation will be secured and instead of being condemned we shall hear those consoling words, "Come, ye blessed of my Father, possess you the kingdom prepared for you from the foundation of the world" (Matt. 25:34).

In order, Christian soul, to obtain the

great favor of a happy death, we must prepare for death all our life, and, so to say, die daily, *quotidie morior,* so that like St. Joseph we may live only in and for Jesus Christ. This practice of dying daily will diminish the terrors of our last day, and change its bitterness, so that it will become the happy day of our deliverance. O Holy Joseph, obtain for me the grace to practice this daily death which will be to me the pledge of a happy eternity.

Second Point.—At the hour of death we shall be protected against the dreaded assaults of the devil by St. Joseph. To reward him for having saved His life from the fury of Herod, Jesus has given him a special power to protect the agonizing from the snares of the devil, and to keep them from eternal perdition. When the holy Patriarch fled into Egypt with the Infant Jesus and Mary the idols fell down, the oracles were silent, the father of lies found himself chained, and the fiends of hell took flight. These are then among the reasons why, throughout the Catholic world, St. Joseph is invoked with Mary as the Patron of a happy death, and it is thus that the devout servants of St. Joseph triumph in their last combat and sleep peacefully in the Lord. Speaking of the last moments of some of her religious who were particularly devoted to St. Joseph, St. Teresa says: "I observed an inexpressible peace and tranquility in them; it seemed as if they entered into ecstasy or the sweet calm of prayer. Exteriorly nothing indicated that any temptations disturbed the interior peace they enjoyed. This heavenly light with which I was favored has had the effect of banishing from my heart the fear of death which I formerly had. It now appears to me that the act of dying is easy for souls who are devoted to St. Joseph."

Christian soul, may these sentiments be ours, may we have the same consolations at our last hour, and may we be able to say with St. Paul: "I have fought a good fight, I have finished my course, I have kept the faith" (2 Tim. 4:7).

PRAYER

Great saint, who art the model and protector of the dying, I implore thee to obtain that I may die the death of the Just. In order to deserve this favor I will begin from this moment to prepare myself for death. Jesus, Mary, Joseph, be merciful now and at the hour of my death. Amen.

EXAMPLE

The Venerable Sister Pudentia Zagnoni who is celebrated in the Franciscan Order for her eminent virtue, had a particular devotion to St. Joseph and received some singularly precious favors from him at the hour of her death. On that trying occasion the Saint appeared and for her greater consolation held in his arms the blessed Infant, Him who forms the joy of angels, the happiness of heaven, the life of pure souls. No words can describe the transports of holy joy which this vision produced in the soul of the dying sister, and the Religious present were m some degree participators in her happiness when they heard her conversing with St. Joseph and the Divine Infant, thanking the former for having changed the bitterness of that dread hour into heavenly sweetness and expressing also her gratitude to the Divine

The Month of St. Joseph

Infant for coming in so loving a form to invite her to the marriage feast which He had prepared in heaven for those whom He had been pleased to dignify by the title of His Spouses. It appeared also to the Religious that St. Joseph placed the Divine Infant in the arms of their dying sister, thus giving her death a closer resemblance to his own at Nazareth; for he had the happy privilege of dying in the sacred arms of Jesus.

TWENTY-SIXTH DAY

ST. JOSEPH IN LIMBO

I. He consoles the souls of the Just.
II. He is chosen the consoler of the souls in Purgatory.

First Point.—The soul of Joseph on leaving his body descended into Limbo, for Heaven was not yet opened. The Venerable Mary of Agreda said, that this glorious Patriarch was destined by the Holy Trinity to preach Jesus Christ to the Saints of the Old Testament who waited for their Deliverer. As daybreak announces the rising sun which dispels the darkness of the night. so did Joseph announce the Divine Sun of Justice who was soon to visit them, and take them with Him into the Heavenly Jerusalem. With what transports of joy did not the Patriarchs and the Prophets and the innumerable souls of the Just welcome the Foster-father of Jesus and the Spouse of Mary, and how great was their happiness to bear him speak of the Redeemer and of Mary His Mother; for who better than he could satisfy their pious curiosity? He had seen everything, and during the thirty years he had passed in the presence of the Son and the Mother he had been the witness of their lives, and could no doubt furnish details that the Apostles have not given to us. Oh! how many secrets did he not divulge to these holy souls, to whom he was not only an evangelist, but a consoling angel.

Christian soul, let us be Apostles also by making Jesus and Mary known to others. They are, alas, but little known in the world, even by those who pass as their disciples. Many there are who deserve the reproof that our Divine Master made the Apostles on the eve of His passion: "So long a time have I been with you and have you not known me?" (John 14:9). Yes, let us make Jesus and Mary known; let us speak of their prerogatives, the blessings they have showered upon us, and their great love for us; for the knowledge of all this will cause others to love and serve them better, and will help to deliver souls from the captivity of sin.

Second Point.—Consider that by his descent into Limbo, and the consolation he then brought the souls who were detained there awaiting their deliverance, St. Joseph has merited the title of Father and Protector of those other souls who are suffering in the flames of Purgatory.

"The Son of God," said a pious author, "having the keys of Heaven, gave one to Mary and another to St. Joseph, so that they might admit their faithful servants." We may then confidently believe that in Heaven our holy Patron will not cease to intercede for the poor souls that are detained by Divine justice in the expiatory flames of Purgatory, and that he often sends ministering angels from Heaven to relieve and deliver them. But if it is true that the holy Patriarch is the consoler of all these captive souls, it is true also that he reserves the more tender marks of his love for those who during life exerted themselves more especially in making known the devotion towards him. The first Joseph relieved all the Egyptians during the prevalence of the famine, by distributing the corn that he had stored, but his generosity was shown more especially to his own brothers. Not satisfied with filling their sacks with corn he gave them back the money they had brought to pay for it. Our glorious Patron will treat his servants not only in like manner, but even more generously; for he will not cease interceding for them with Jesus and Mary until he has delivered them from their suffering, and placed them in a place of resplendent light and peace.

Let us also relieve the holy souls of Purgatory. It is a duty that justice, charity, and gratitude, require of us. Christian soul, recall to your remembrance the many proofs of tender love that a father, mother, brother, and sister have given you. Can you forget them now when in their place of suffering they stretch forth their hands in supplication towards you. Hasten to procure a speedy deliverance for them by the Sacrifice of the Mass, by Holy Communion, and through the intercession of St. Joseph.

PRAYER

Sweet Jesus, have mercy on the souls of the dead who in life have not entirely satisfied Thy justice for their sins; shorten the time of their sufferings, and hear the prayers that we address to Thee through the intercession of St. Joseph. O Jesus, grant them eternal rest. Amen.

EXAMPLE

Father Evangelista, of the Society of Jesus, one of the most devoted clients of St. Joseph, obtained through his intercession the following singular favor.

For more than twenty years this great servant of God endured most excruciating pains from asthma. The thought struck him, how comparatively light these sufferings would be, were he only certain after death of enjoying God. On the 19th March, 1626, he humbly begged of God, through the intercession of St. Joseph, to grant him the assurance of eternal salvation. Animated with the liveliest confidence, that he should obtain the favor he so earnestly desired, he prepared to celebrate the Holy Sacrifice of the Mass, and his confidence increased, when he found he had been appointed to say Mass at the altar of the Saint. Scarcely had he begun the Holy Sacrifice, when he felt his soul inflamed with so tender a devotion, that be remained wrapped in the contemplation of the glory with which the saints are rewarded in Heaven. The feelings of humility, gratitude, and love, with which his heart then overflowed, left him motionless and unable to proceed. Having at length come to himself, he made an entire oblation of his whole being to God and to St. Joseph, and continued the Mass, as well as his feelings would permit him, until the consecration of the chalice; but after having pronounced with tender devotion the words *qui pro vobis* (which for you) he heard distinctly an interior voice, and this consoling word *efficaciter* (efficaciously), after which he proceeded repeating the usual form, *et pro multis effundetur in remissionem peccatorum* (which shall be shed for you and for many to the remission of sin). What must have been the feelings of holy joy, which inundated the soul of this holy man, at the intimation that the blood of Jesus Christ had been efficaciously shed for him, and that his salvation was secured. During the seventeen years Father Evangelista survived, the mere recollection of this great favor filled his soul with heavenly delight, and made him happy amidst his greatest sufferings.

TWENTY-SEVENTH DAY

THE RESURRECTION OF JOSEPH

I. Resurrection most probable.
II. Resurrection most glorious.

First Point.—The resurrection of St. Joseph and his ascension into Heaven with our Lord are pious beliefs which the Church does not forbid. And who could have a better claim to accompany Christ in His triumph than St. Joseph? Joseph who had so lovingly accompanied Him in His exile into Egypt and in the laborious pilgrimage of His life. "If," said St. Bernardine of Siena, "the Redeemer willed out of filial piety, to glorify the body as well as the soul of the ever Blessed Virgin on the day of her Assumption, one can and one ought piously to believe that He did not do less for St. Joseph, who is so great amongst all the saints, and that He raised him gloriously the same day He arose Himself.

Reflect, Christian soul, that we shall all rise again at the end of the world, which is a most consoling article of our faith. *Credo carnis resurrectionem.* Our body which has suffered will rise in glory. Each of us can exclaim, in the fervor of our faith and love, "I know that my Redeemer liveth, and in the last day that I shall rise out of the earth" (Job, 19:25).

Second Point.—We read in Scripture that the guardian of his God will be glorified, and these words seem to have been inspired by the Holy Ghost to predict the glorification of St. Joseph. We can dwell in thought on the angel's greeting and the words of Jesus: "Come, good and faithful servant, the blessed of my heavenly Father, come, faithful guardian, take possession of the kingdom that you have merited; for 1 was naked on the earth and you clothed me, I was hungry and you gave me to eat, I was thirsty and you gave me to drink, I was a stranger and you took me in; enter now into the joy of the Lord." O sweet Jesus, be forever blest for having willed to honor so greatly in heaven him who loved Thee so tenderly on earth, him we also wish to honor and love with all our hearts.

If we wish to merit a glorious resurrection we must value and preserve our chastity; this beautiful virtue, as Tertullian expresses it, renders our flesh angelic, *Angelificata caro*, and enriches it with the seeds of a glorious immortality. "Blessed are the clean of heart for they shall see God" (Matt. 5:8), and one day they will shine like stars in the firmament.

PRAYER

I rejoice, O St. Joseph, my holy Protector, that it is permitted to believe that thou art in Heaven in soul and body. I rejoice in thy glorious resurrection, and I beseech thee to obtain a great desire for me of my heavenly country, and that one day I may witness thy triumph and thank Jesus that thou hast been so glorified. Amen.

The Month of St. Joseph

EXAMPLE

A girl nineteen years of age called Philomena, who had been suffering some time from a nervous illness, was obliged on September the 5th, 1867, to keep her bed, as the slightest movement caused agonies of pain, and her digestive organs were so impaired that she could not retain even a spoonful of broth. The remedies prescribed by physicians being of no avail, her only hope of relief was from God, and those who visited her prayed that He would have pity on her, and reward the patience with which she suffered, by taking her to Heaven.

No change occurred and she was still in this suffering state when, on the 28th of February, she received a letter from the Superior of the convent in which she had been educated, who urged her not to despair, but to begin a novena to St. Joseph on the 10th of March, which would end on the Feast of the great Patriarch. The confidence of the Superior was so great that she ended her letter with these words: "I feel so confident, that I will only add goodbye till we meet again. I look forward to a visit from you on the 19th; our Convent as you know is under

The Month of St. Joseph

the patronage of St. Joseph."

The confidence with which the Superior was inspired was shared by the invalid, who told all who came to see her that she would be cured on the 19th. During the Novena the sufferings of the poor girl increased and on the 17th she was in great agony. The next day a slight amelioration was perceptible, and on the 19th she was able to receive Holy Communion. A few minutes after she rose from her bed and prostrated herself before the statue of St. Joseph, which stood on a table near. Her cure was not only instantaneous but complete, and all bad symptoms without a single exception disappeared. Philomena, who ever after enjoyed good health, used to say that all things could be obtained from St, Joseph on the day of his feast.

TWENTY-EIGHTH DAY

ST. JOSEPH IN HEAVEN

I. His glory.
II. His happiness.

First Point.—In proportion as Joseph humbled himself in this world he is exalted in glory in Heaven. While on earth he was as the last of men, in Heaven he is next to Jesus and Mary. On earth he suffered the most abject poverty, in Heaven he is in the possession of everything, and with Mary is the dispenser of the Divine treasures. On earth he had to depend on everybody, in Heaven he is treated with honor, and commands rather than petitions. He is an object of complacency to the Holy Family, to the Father of whom he is the image on earth, to the Son whom he fed with the labor of his hands, to the Holy Ghost whose inspirations he followed faithfully. Mary the Queen of

The Month of St. Joseph

Heaven regards him with tenderness, the angels and saints rejoice in his triumph. Thus is honor given to him whom the King of kings has honored. The great Theologian Suarez exclaimed: "O Joseph, how great is your glory in Heaven; you surpass all the saints in grace and beatitude!"

When will it be given to us to see and contemplate the glory of our dear Patron in Heaven, and to partake of the happiness that he prepares for his servants. O glorious St. Joseph, we are alone, poor, and in exile in an enemy's country, where each day we have fresh combats; console us in our exile, lessen our afflictions, and guide our frail barque on the stormy sea of this world until it reaches the shores of our heavenly country.

Second Point.—St. Joseph's happiness in Heaven equals his glory. The possession of Jesus and Mary when on earth formed his joy; *Constituit eum principem omnis possessionis suæ.*

It is still this glorious prerogative which St. Bernardine of Siena assures forms his supreme beatitude in heaven. What unutterable happiness must it be for this blessed Father to see in all the magnificence of His glory the God whom he had seen so lowly in the days of His mortal life laid upon straw and passing his days unnoticed in a poor workshop. More privileged than any of the saints he loves Jesus not only as his God, but he continues to love Him as his Son. What joy also is it not to him to see Mary his August Spouse seated on a resplendent throne on the right hand of Jesus; but to form a true idea of how much the happiness of the Immaculate Virgin increases that of St. Joseph, we should love her as he loved her, and we should have shared with him the trials and humiliations of this holy Mother.

Prostrate at thy feet, O glorious St. Joseph, I praise God for having raised thee to such a high degree of glory, and for the torrents of delights with which He has filled thy heart. Thou art in thy true country, whilst I thy child mourn in exile; thou hast reached the port whilst I thy child am still tossed on the stormy sea of the world. Oh, save me from being lost, thou who didst save the Divine Infant from the fury of Herod, and conduct me to Jesus and Mary where I shall share thy happiness.

Christian soul, never forget that it rests with yourself to share with St. Joseph the joys of heaven.

PRAYER

O Blessed Joseph, it is thy love for Jesus and Mary which has merited thee so high a degree of glory and happiness. O loving Father, I am thy child; obtain grace for me to walk in thy footsteps, to love Jesus and His holy Mother as thou didst love them, and to be united to them with thee in a happy eternity. Amen.

EXAMPLE

In the month of April, 1862, the Superior of the Little Sisters of the Poor in the city of Lyons found the sheets belonging to the beds for the old men were so worn that they could not be used any longer. The procurator's purse was empty and she was at a loss how to procure new ones. The Sister Superior remembering that she had often obtained favors through the intercession of St. Joseph, folded one of the old sheets and placed it at the foot of the statue of the glorious Patriarch imploring him not to forget the poor who had been confided to her care.

The Month of St. Joseph

The following day a young man on horseback called and asked to see the Sister Superior. When she came be handed her a sum of money, saying, "This is to buy sheets for your poor men." The sister was overjoyed, her confidence in St. Joseph had been well rewarded.

TWENTY-NINTH DAY

ST. JOSEPH, PATRON OF THE UNIVERSAL CHURCH

I. Patron of great power.
II. Patron of great goodness.

First Point.—The Sovereign Pontiff Pius IX, yielding to the wish of great numbers of Bishops and of many of the laity, deemed it advisable in the trying times in which we live, to give the barque of Peter a protector, and he solemnly declared St. Joseph to be the Patron of the Universal Church. And whom could he have named as a more powerful protector? Jesus to whom all power had been given in Heaven and on earth, had vouchsafed to be born subject to him and to obey him during thirty years. His prayer which was all-powerful on earth will not be less so now that he is in Heaven; and the

Church proves what she thinks of the power of her August Protector when she asks through his intercession what she cannot obtain for herself. The learned Dominican, Isidore de l'Isle, had previously given him the title of Patron of the Church Militant, *Patronus militantis Ecclesiæ*; and St. Thomas Aquinas assures us that his patronage extends to both our spiritual and our temporal necessities.

"Some saints," said he, "have received the privilege of protecting us more especially under certain circumstances, but to St. Joseph it has been given to help us in all our necessities, and to defend, to protect, and watch with paternal affection over all those who have recourse to him."

Christian soul, in these days of great trial, let us with great confidence have recourse to our powerful Protector, and let us beseech him to watch over the Church which is so sorely tried. Pius IX. has said that Mary and Joseph, the two great supports of the Church, are retaking in the heart of man the place which they should never have lost, and that the world would be saved again.

Second Point.—If St. Joseph is regarded as

The Month of St. Joseph

the most powerful, he is also the most compassionate Protector. No other Saint loves the Church as he loves it; for no other is so closely connected with it. According to St. Paul the other Saints form as it were the body of Jesus Christ; they are His members and the members of one another, but St. Joseph looks upon all the faithful as his children. His most ardent desire is to protect them; for there is no one who is not an object of his solicitude. Let us then have recourse to him with great confidence and he will protect us. "I do not remember," said St. Teresa, "to have ever asked him for anything that he has not granted."

Yes, Christian soul, let us kneel at the feet of Joseph and pay homage to a power that knows no limits, and to a goodness which embraces all mankind. Let us in future invoke him oftener and with more confidence. Would that we could make use of the voice of all created beings, and say to everyone: "Take Joseph for your chief Patron, for the most intimate of your friends, for the most powerful of your protectors."

The Month of St. Joseph

PRAYER

Thy power and thy goodness encourage me to have recourse to thee, O holy Joseph. I come to thee with the confidence of a child who goes to the best of fathers; protect me, protect the Universal Church which forms thy family, and protect the Pope, Christ's Vicar on earth, Amen.

EXAMPLE

When the revolution broke out in Rome, in 1848, the Religious of the Order of St. Joseph, whose Convent was situated in the Campo Vaccino, were in the greatest alarm. Feeling that they could not hope for any human assistance, they had recourse to St. Joseph, and prayed fervently to their powerful Protector. As the danger increased so did their confidence in their loving Father. The roar of the cannon day and night filled their hearts with terror; for several houses near had been destroyed, killing in their fall many people, and they momentarily expected their Convent would share the same fate. "If

The Month of St. Joseph

it is God's will that we should be killed, said they, His will be done, but let us die in the chapel."

They all accordingly took refuge there; it was the middle of the night, and after praying a long time, overcome by terror and fatigue, they fell asleep. Day broke before they awoke from their sleep, which had been so profound, that neither the roar of the cannon, the exploding of shells, or the falling of the houses had been able to wake them. St. Joseph had watched over them during that terrible night, and they fervently returned thanks for such a signal mark of his protection.

On another occasion during the siege a shell fell in the middle of their workroom, and they gave themselves up for lost, but the Spouse of Mary, their special Patron, again protected them. To their astonishment, in a manner that could not be explained, the shell rose from the spot on which it had fallen, and passing out of the window, fell and exploded on the other side of the street, without causing any damage or loss of life. This prodigy was witnessed by many persons who could not sufficiently express their surprise. The Superior caused the exploded shell to be

The Month of St. Joseph

brought into the Convent, and placed as a votive offering before the Statue of St. Joseph.

THIRTIETH DAY

THE EXCELLENCE OF DEVOTION TO ST. JOSEPH

I. It has been in a particular way reserved for the present time.
II. It answers most admirably the needs of the present times.

First Point.—God permitted that the first Joseph, the son of the Patriarch Jacob, should be imprisoned for a long time in a dark prison, from whence he was liberated with honor. Something similar is seen in the ways of Providence with regard to the second Joseph, the Foster-father of Jesus. For many centuries St. Joseph was little known in Christendom. God in His wisdom reserved the wider knowledge of this devotion for the days of trial and for the last combats of the Church. At the present time devotion to St.

The Month of St. Joseph

Joseph has become more known; it expands, spreads rapidly, and promises the most abundant blessings. How many churches, chapels, and altars have been erected in honor of St. Joseph; how many confraternities and congregations have been placed under his patronage; and of late one entire month of the year has been set apart to honor him in a special manner. Many are the souls who daily pay him a tribute of veneration, confidence, and love. The Church which by inspiration of Divine wisdom had allowed the holy Patriarch to remain undistinguished among the host of saints, manifests him to the whole world in these our days in all the splendor of his greatness, and bids all her children go to Joseph, *Ite ad Joseph.* Go to him with confidence, for he has been proclaimed the Protector of the great Catholic family, and celebrate his Feast henceforth with the pomp and solemnity due to the Prince and Master of the House of the Lord.

Christian soul, let us bless God for so providentially making known the devotion to our much-loved Patron, and let us endeavor to spread this devotion as much as possible. Yes, let us be in future zealous apostles and fervent servants of St. Joseph. At the hour of our death what a consolation will it not be to us to have made known the Foster-father of Jesus, the Spouse of Mary, and the Patron of the Universal Church.

Second Point.—What more fitting devotion could there be than that to St. Joseph in the troubled times in which we live? Three great evils undermine society and afflict the Church: the disorganization of families, the love of pleasure, and the disorganization of the working class. The most efficacious remedy for these three wounds is devotion to St. Joseph. To the heads of families who have let authority fall from their hands, and to children who shake off the paternal yoke, we show them St. Joseph, the model of fathers of families, and Jesus who was always submissive to him. To the present generation, who seek only for gratification and pleasure, who work only to procure enjoyment, we give St. Joseph to them also for their model, the man pre-eminently just, chaste, disinterested, poor, and leading a hidden life in his workshop; and finally, to poor workmen we offer St. Joseph as their Patron. He was himself a workman, whose only aim was to lead an interior and humble life, entirely devoted to the service of God in the company of Jesus and Mary.

Since devotion to this great Saint is so suited to our necessities, and since God constituted Joseph the master of His house, as in previous ages He had made the ancient Patriarch master over the land of Egypt, so that food was secured for the people of Israel, let us imitate the sons of Jacob, and if we do not wish to die let us go to Joseph. A great scarcity devastates the world, and the food that is wanting is not only the bread that supports our bodies, but it is the living bread which feeds our souls, it is the truth which enlightens and grace which sanctifies. Yes, let us go to Joseph and he will give us Jesus Christ, the wheat of the elect, the sacred bread of travelers.

PRAYER

Full well do we understand, O glorious Patriarch, the need the present age has of thy protection, in order to cure evil and enable men to save their souls. We resolve to love

The Month of St. Joseph

thee more, to pray to thee with more confidence, and to use our endeavors to induce others to love and pray to thee; and do thou, O holy Joseph, impart us thy paternal blessing.

EXAMPLE

St. Joseph has been regarded by many devout souls as the Patron of travelers, and the following incident is a striking example of this pious belief.

A young man belonging to the merchant service received orders to proceed from Havre to Marseilles. Before leaving his native town his sister, when bidding him farewell, put a small statue of St. Joseph in his coat-pocket, at the same time praying the great Saint to bless his voyage and bring him back safe and sound. When the ship was off Cadiz, the captain ordered the young sailor to tighten a rope aloft. Whilst executing the order, the rope, which proved to be rotten, broke, and he fell unperceived into the sea. Being a good swimmer, be tried to regain the vessel, but it was in vain, and already was his strength beginning to fail when he remembered his sister's prayer and the little

The Month of St. Joseph

statue she had given him of St. Joseph. The recollection seemed to give him new strength, he invoked his heavenly Protector with faith and confidence and promised to have Mass offered in his honor if his life was saved. His prayer was immediately granted, for an invisible hand seemed to support him on the waves till he was able to grasp the rope which had by that time been thrown to him from the vessel. On his return to Havre the young sailor hastened to fulfil his promise, and together with his family assisted at a Mass offered in thanksgiving to St. Joseph for the visible protection he had vouchsafed to him.

Let us pray also to this great Saint, and beseech him to bless our journeys and defend us from all dangers.

THIRTY-FIRST DAY

PRACTICES IN HONOR OF ST. JOSEPH

I. Daily practices.
II. Weekly practices.
III. Yearly practices.

First Point.—We have now come to the last day of the Month of March, a month consecrated to St. Joseph, which has been so full of consolation to us. But before it closes, we must make some practical resolutions which will help us to persevere in devotion, love, and veneration to our holy Patron. Let us resolve to let no day pass without offering up some prayer in his honor, and let us acquire the habit of repeating the names of Jesus, Mary, and Joseph, every morning on rising, and every night when retiring to rest. These holy names will serve also as an ejaculatory prayer during the course of the day, and more especially in time of temptation and danger, or again, when we feel called upon to make some sacrifice which it costs to make. St. Gertrude in a vision saw the souls in Heaven bow reverently when the religious pronounced the name of Joseph when reciting office in choir. Let us represent to ourselves our Guardian Angel bowing also with respect and love each time we devoutly repeat this blessed name.

Second Point.—Let us resolve, in union with a number of devout Christians who honor St. Joseph, to set apart the Wednesday of each week to pray more particularly, and to render special homage to this great Saint. Friday is consecrated to the Sacred Heart, Saturday to the Blessed Virgin, and Wednesday to St. Joseph. Hear Mass that day in his honor, and if unable to go to Communion make a Spiritual Communion. Our Lord made known to one of the Saints how pleasing these Spiritual Communions are to Him, and this was signified by showing two precious vases, one of gold and the other of silver, and the Saint was given to understand that the golden vase contained Sacramental Communions, and the silver vase Spiritual Communions. Let us also endeavor to make some interior or exterior act of mortification every Wednesday, or give an alms, or perform some good work in honor of St. Joseph.

Third Point.—Our last resolution must be that of faithfully celebrating every year the Month of St. Joseph. How many graces and how many blessings does not this Month procure for us. The daily exercises will help us to sanctify Lent, and to prepare for our Easter Communion. It is also a very beneficial practice to set apart one day in each month to make a little retreat. The Feast of St. Joseph, the 19th March, must not be passed without some preparation; this can be done by making a Novena, and terminating it by receiving Holy Communion in his honor. If we are able to bestow an alms, it will be well to give it that day to three people, in honor of the three members of the Holy Family.

These, O Christian soul, are the resolutions we will offer this day before the Altar of St. Joseph, whilst concluding the

The Month of St. Joseph

devotions of the Month. May we keep them with courage and perseverance! They will be a pledge of our love and devotion to our Father and Protector, and for us they will be a source of abundant blessings. Let us place them in St. Joseph's hands, and beseech him to obtain grace for us to keep them faithfully.

EXAMPLE

A priest who was on the African Mission, in the year 1867, relates a striking instance of the way in which St. Joseph hears prayers that are addressed to him. The missioner had received orders from his Bishop to make a visitation of the whole district under his charge, but, owing to circumstances, not being able to do so at the usual time of the year, he was obliged to undertake the journey in a time of great drought, which made traveling extremely difficult, owing to the scarcity of fodder for the mules. In South Africa there is no grass, only a sort of bush, like heath, on which the animals feed. The Father started on his journey, and had only been gone a day, when an old Italian cobbler arrived at the mission house, having walked

The Month of St. Joseph

a hundred and fifty miles in order to receive the Sacraments, for he felt his days were numbered. He was a cripple, having met with an accident which had broken his back, and caused him to be bent nearly double, so that in walking he was obliged to rest his hands on his knees. In this painful position the old man had walked the one hundred and fifty miles, many days and nights being spent on the road. On his arrival be asked to see the Priest; a lay brother replied that the Missioner had left on the previous day, and it was impossible to say when he would return. The cobbler was sadly disappointed; he said he had not been able to go to Confession for years, and had only lately heard that there was a Missioner at Oudtshoorn.

After waiting a few days he left in despair, walking back the one hundred and fifty miles to his home. Meanwhile, the Missioner pushed forward on his journey, but the drought was so terrible, and the mules became so weak, that he was obliged to stop. The district in which he found himself was wholly unknown to him, and he had no guide but a compass; seeing a hill not far off, he climbed it, hoping to see from the summit some sign of a human dwelling. To his great

The Month of St. Joseph

joy he descried a Dutch or Boer farm, and returning to his mules, he managed to get them as far as the farm house. On knocking at the door, the farmer came out, and asked him who he was, and what he wanted. The Missioner replied that he was a Catholic Priest visiting his district, but owing to the drought, he could not get on, for there was no water for his mules. The farmer, on hearing that he was a Catholic Priest, told him he was himself a Protestant, but that there was a Catholic who had been many years on the farm, an old Italian cobbler, who was in a dying state, and he offered to conduct him to him, The Father followed his guide, who took him to an outhouse where the dying cobbler was laid, and whose joy was great at this unexpected visit of a Priest. He heard his Confession, passed the night with him in the outhouse, and next morning arranged a little altar, said Mass, and administered Communion and Extreme Unction. In the course of the day the poor old cobbler died; he told the Missioner, that taught by his pious Mother, he had said every day, "St. Joseph, pray for me, that I may die well." His prayer had not

passed unheard. For St. Joseph had sent

The Month of St. Joseph

across the burning sands of Africa a Priest to hear his Confession, and give him the last Sacraments, enabling him thus to die well.

Let us, before the close of this month, resolve to follow the example of the poor cobbler, and never retire to rest without saying, as he did: "St. Joseph, pray for me, that I may die well."

🕮 LITANY OF ST. JOSEPH

Lord, have mercy on us.
Christ, have mercy on us.
Lord, have mercy on us.
Christ, hear us.
Christ, graciously hear us.
God, the Son, Redeemer of the world, *have mercy on us.*
God, the Holy Ghost, *have mercy on us.*
Holy Trinity, one God, *have mercy on us.*
Holy Mary, *pray for us.*
Holy Joseph, *pray for us.*
Noble scion of David, *pray for us.*
Light of the Patriarchs, *pray for us.*
Spouse of the Mother of God, *pray for us.*
Chaste guardian of the Virgin, *pray for us.*
Foster-father of the Son of God, *pray for us.*
Sedulous defender of Christ, *pray for us.*
Head of the Holy Family, *pray for us.*
Joseph most just, *pray for us.*
Joseph most chaste, *pray for us.*
Joseph most prudent, *pray for us.*
Joseph most valiant, *pray for us.*
Joseph most obedient, *pray for us.*
Joseph most faithful, *pray for us.*
Mirror of patience, *pray for us.*
Lover of poverty, *pray for us.*

The Month of St. Joseph

Model of poverty, *pray for us.*
Model of workers, *pray for us.*
Ornament of domestic life, *pray for us.*
Hope of the sick, *pray for us.*
Patron of the dying *pray for us.*
Terror of the demons, *pray for us.*
Protector of the holy Church, *pray for us.*

Lamb of God, Who takest away the sins of the world,
> *Spare us, O Lord!*

Lamb of God, Who takest away the sins of the world,
> *Graciously hear us, O Lord!*

Lamb of God, Who takest away the sins of the world,
> *Have mercy on us, O Lord!*

℣. He made him master of his house
℟. And ruler of all his possessions.

Let us pray

O God, who in Thy ineffable Providence didst vouchsafe to choose blessed Joseph to be the spouse of Thy most holy Mother; grant, we beseech Thee, that we may have him whom we venerate as our protector on

The Month of St. Joseph

earth, as our intercessor in heaven. Who livest and reignest world without end. Amen.

The Month of St. Joseph

🖋 MARCH DEVOTIONS

INDULGENCES

Three hundred days, each day.

Plenary, on any one day on the usual conditions.

The month may be either that of March or a month terminating on the feast of St. Joseph, March 19.

Persons legitimately hindered from practicing this devotion in March may substitute any other month.

The devotion consists of any prayers or other pious practice in honor of the saint.

—Pius IX, April 27, 1865; July 18, 1877.

ACT OF CONSECRATION TO ST. JOSEPH.

O glorious St. Joseph, chosen by God to be the reputed father of Jesus, the most pure spouse of Mary ever Virgin, and the head of the Holy Family, and then elected by the Vicar of Christ to be the heavenly Patron and Protector of the Church founded by Jesus Christ; with the greatest confidence I implore at this time thy powerful aid for the entire Church militant. Protect in a special manner with thy truly paternal love the Supreme

The Month of St. Joseph

Pontiff and all the bishops and priests united to the See of St. Peter. Defend all those who labor for souls in the midst of the afflictions and tribulations of this life, and obtain the willing submission of every nation throughout the world to the Church, the necessary means of salvation for all.

O dearest St. Joseph, be pleased to accept the consecration which I make to thee of myself. I dedicate myself entirely to thee that thou mayest ever be my father, my protector, and my guide in the way of salvation. Obtain for me great purity of heart and a fervent love of the interior life. Grant that after thy example all my actions may be directed to the greater glory of God, in union with the divine Heart of Jesus and the immaculate heart of Mary, and with thee. Finally, pray for me that I may be able to share in the peace and joy of thy most holy death. Amen.

Indulgence of 300 days, one a day.
—Leo XIII, July 18, 1885.

The Month of St. Joseph

INDULGENCED PRAYERS IN HONOR OF ST. JOSEPH FOR THOSE IN THEIR AGONY

Eternal Father, by Thy love for St. Joseph, whom Thou didst select from among all men to represent Thee upon earth, have mercy on us and on the dying.
Our Father, Hail Mary, Glory be to the Father.

Eternal divine Son, by Thy love for St. Joseph, who was Thy faithful guardian upon earth, have mercy upon us and upon the dying.
Our Father, Hail Mary, Glory be to the Father.

Eternal divine Spirit, by Thy love for St. Joseph, who so carefully watched over Mary, Thy beloved spouse, have mercy on us and on the dying.
Our Father, Hail Mary, Glory be to the Father.

Indulgence of 300 days, one a day.
—Leo XIII, May 17, 1884.

The Month of St. Joseph

St. Joseph, reputed Father of our Lord, Jesus Christ, and true spouse of Mary, ever Virgin, pray for us.
>Indulgence of 300 days, once a day.
>—Leo XIII, May 15 1891

St. Joseph, model and patron of those who love the Sacred Heart of Jesus, pray for us.
>Indulgence of 100 days, once a day.
>—Leo XIII, Dec. 19 1891

St. Joseph, friend of the Sacred Heart, pray for us.
>Indulgence of 100 days, once a day.
>—Pius XI

Jesus, Mary, Joseph, I give you my heart and my soul.
Jesus, Mary, Joseph, assist me in my last agony.
Jesus, Mary, Joseph, may I breathe forth my soul in peace with you.
>Indulgence of 300 days for all three, each time they are said.
>—Pius VII, Aug. 26, 1814

The Month of St. Joseph

MEMORARE IN HONOR OF ST. JOSEPH

REMEMBER, O most pure spouse of the Blessed Virgin Mary, my sweet Protector, St. Joseph: that no one ever had recourse to thy protection or implored thy aid without obtaining relief. Confiding, therefore, in thy goodness, I come before thee and humbly beg thee. Despise not my petitions, Foster-father fo my Redeemer, but graciously receive them. Amen.

Indulgence of 300 days, once a day.
—Pius IX, June 26, 1863.

PRAYERS TO ST. JOSEPH

St. Joseph, whose protection is to great, so strong, so prompt before the throne of God, I place in thee all my interest and desires. O St. Joseph, do assist us by thy power and protection, and obtain for us from thy Divine Son, all spiritual blessings through Jesus Christ, Our Lord, so that having engaged here below your heavenly powers, I may

offer my thanksgiving and homage to the most loving of fathers.

O St. Joseph, I never weary contemplating you with Jesus asleep in your arms. I dare not approach while He reposes near your heart. Press Him in my name, and kiss His fine head for me, so He may return that kiss when I draw my dying breath.

St. Joseph, Patron of departing souls, pray for us.

PRAYER FOR A HAPPY DEATH

O Blessed Joseph, who yielded thy last breath in the arms of Jesus and of Mary, when God will send death to end our career of life, come Holy Father with Jesus and Mary to aid us, and obtain this grace for us, to accept death with perfect resignation to God's holy will, and in union with the bitter death of Jesus, that by our death we may atone for our own sins and help the other poor dying sinners. Let us all die in the sweet embrace of Jesus and of Mary. Into your sacred hands, Jesus, Mary, Joseph, we live and dying, commend our souls. Amen.

HYMN OF PRAISE TO ST. JOSEPH

From the Greek Menæa on the Sunday following Christmas

OSEPH, the Spouse, saw with his own eyes the fulfillment of what the Prophets had foretold. He was destined for an espousal, such as no other mortal had, and he received the revelation from Angels, saying: Glory be to the Lord, for he hath given peace to the earth!

Tell, O Joseph, to David, the ancestor of God our Savior, the prodigies thou hast seen. Thou hast seen the Virgin holding the Infant in her arms; thou didst adore with the Magi; thou didst unite with the Shepherds in giving glory to God, according to the word of the Angels. Do thou beseech Christ our Lord, that he save us.

The infinite God, before whom the powers of heaven tremble, Him, O Joseph, didst thou receive into thy arms, when he was born of the Virgin. Thou wast

The Month of St. Joseph

consecrated by the holy contact; therefore do we honor thee.

Thy spirit was one that was obedient to the divine commands, and thy purity was without reproach; therefore, O blessed Joseph, didst thou receive as thy Spouse her that was pure and immaculate among women. Thou wast the guardian of the chaste Virgin, when she became the worthy tabernacle of the Creator.

To Gabriel alone in heaven, and to thee alone, O blessed Joseph, most worthy of praise, was entrusted, after the spotless Virgin, that great and venerable mystery, which brought the downfall of the cruel prince of darkness.

Thou, O Joseph, the minister of the incomprehensible mystery! in order that the darkness of idolatry might be dispelled, didst lead from the city of David into Egypt the pure Mother, who, like a mysterious cloud, held the Sun hidden in her bosom.

O prudent Joseph! thou, angel-like, didst minister to the Incarnate God when he had reached the age of boyhood. His spiritual rays came direct upon thee, O blessed one! and enlightened thee. Thy heart and soul were bathed in light.

He that, by his only word, made heaven and earth and sea, was called "the Carpenter' Son," yes, thine, O Joseph, that deservest all our admiration. Thou wast called the "Father" of Him that had no beginning, and receivedst from him the glory of being minister of unfathomable mysteries.

Oh! how precious, in the sight of the Lord, was thy death, O blessed Joseph! for thou wast consecrated to him from thine infancy, and wast the holy guardian of the Blessed Virgin. Thou didst thus sing together with her: Let ever creature bless the Lord, and praise him above all for endless ages. Amen.

TE JOSEPH CELEBRENT
Hymn of the Roman Breviary

AY the heavenly host praise thee, O Joseph! My the choirs of Christendom resound with thy name, for great are thy merits, who wast united by a chaste alliance to the Holy Virgin.

Seeing that thy Spouse was soon to be a

The Month of St. Joseph

Mother, a cruel doubt afflicts thy heart; but an Angel visits thee, telling thee that she had conceived of the Holy Ghost the Child she bore in her womb.

When Jesus was born, thou hadst to take him in thine arms, and go with the little fugitive to Egypt's distant land. When he was lost in Jerusalem, thou didst seek after him; and having found him, thy tears were mingled with joy.

Other Saints receive their beatitude after death, when a holy death has crowned their life; they receive their glory, when they have won the palm: but thou, by a strangely happy lot, hadst, even during life, what the Blessed have in heaven,—thou hadst the sweet society of thy God.

O Sovereign Trinity! have mercy on us thy suppliants, and may the intercession of Joseph aid us to reach heaven; that there we may sing to thee our eternal hymn of grateful love. Amen.

The Month of St. Joseph

PRAYER OF PRAISE TO ST. JOSEPH

WE PRAISE and glorify thee, O happy Saint! We hail thee as the Spouse of the Queen of heaven, and Foster-Father of our Redeemer. These titles, which would seem too grand for any human being to enjoy, are thine; and they are but the expression of the dignities conferred on thee by God. The Church of heaven admires the sublime favors thou hast received; the Church on earth joyfully celebrates thy glories, and blesses thee for the favors thou art so unceasingly bestowing upon her.

Though born of the kingly race of David, thou wast the humblest of men; thy spirit led thee to seek obscurity, and a hidden life was thine ambition: but God chose thee to be an instrument in the sublimest of all his works. A noble Virgin of the same family of David—the object of heaven's admiration and the glory and hope of the world—yes, this Virgin is to be thy Spouse. The Holy Ghost is to dwell within her as in a most pure tabernacle; it is to thee, the just and chaste, that he entrusts her as an inestimable treasure. Espouse, then, to thyself her whose beauty the very King of heaven so greatly desires.

The Son of God comes down to this earth, that He may live the life of man; He comes that he may sanctify the ties and affections of kindred. He calls thee Father; He obeys thy orders. What strange emotions must have filled thy heart, O Joseph! when, knowing the prerogatives of thy Spouse and the divinity of thy adopted Son, thou hadst to be the head of this Family, which united heaven and earth into one! What respectful and tender love for Mary, thy Blessed Spouse! What gratitude and profound worship of Jesus, who obeyed thee as thy Child! O mysteries of Nazareth! a God dwells among men, and permits Himself to be called the Son of Joseph!

O sublime minister of the greatest of blessings, intercede for us with God made Man. Ask him to bestow Humility upon us—that holy virtue which raised thee to such exalted dignity, and which must be the basis of our conversion. It was pride that led us into sin and made us prefer our own will to that of God: yet will he pardon us if we offer him the sacrifice of a contrite and humbled heart. Get us this virtue, without

The Month of St. Joseph

which there can be no true penance. Pray also for us, O Joseph, that we may be chaste. Without purity of mind and body, we cannot come nigh the God of all sanctity, who suffers nothing defiled to approach him. He wills to make our bodies, by his grace, the temples of his holy Spirit: do thou, great Saint, help us to maintain ourselves in so exalted a dignity, or to recover it, if we have lost it.

And lastly, O Faithful Spouse of Mary! recommend us to our Mother. If she cast a look of pity upon us during these days of reconciliation, we shall be saved: for she is the Queen of Mercy, and Jesus, her Son, will pardon us and change our hearts, if she intercede for us, O Joseph! Remind her of Bethlehem, Egypt, and Nazareth, in all of which she received from thee such marks of thy devotedness. Tell her, that we, also, love and honor thee; and Mary will reward us for our devotion to him that was given her by heaven as her protector and support.

www.ingramcontent.com/pod-product-compliance
Lightning Source LLC
Chambersburg PA
CBHW021442070526
44577CB00002B/255